GW00838505

Non-League Football Supporters' Guide & Yearbook 2013

EDITOR
John Robinson

Twenty-first Edition

For details of our range of 2,000 books and over 400 DVDs, visit our web site or contact us using the information shown below.

British Library Cataloguing in Publication Data
A catalogue record for this book is available from the British Library

ISBN: 978-1-86223-239-6

Copyright © 2012, SOCCER BOOKS LIMITED (01472 696226)
72 St. Peter's Avenue, Cleethorpes, N.E. Lincolnshire, DN35 8HU, England

Web site www.soccer-books.co.uk • e-mail info@soccer-books.co.uk

Manufactured in the UK by T.J. International Ltd, Padstow

FOREWORD

Our thanks go to the numerous club officials who have aided us in the compilation of information contained in this guide and also to Michael Robinson (page layouts), Bob Budd (cover artwork), Tony Brown (Cup Statistics – www.soccerdata.com) and Derek Mead for providing some of the photographs.

Any readers who have up-to-date ground photographs which they would like us to consider for use in a future edition of this guide are requested to contact us at our address which is shown on the facing page.

The fixtures listed later in this book were released just a short time before we went to print and, as such, some of the dates shown may be subject to change. We therefore suggest that readers treat these fixtures as a rough guide and check dates carefully before attending matches.

Finally, we would like to wish our readers a safe and happy spectating season.

John Robinson
EDITOR

CONTENTS

THE FOOTBALL CONFERENCE BLUE SQUARE PREMIER

Address   Third Floor, Wellington House, 31-34 Waterloo Street, Birmingham   B2 5TJ

Phone (0121) 214-1950

Web site www.footballconference.co.uk

Clubs for the 2012/2013 Season

AFC TELFORD UNITED

Founded: 2004
Former Names: Formed after Telford United FC went out of business. TUFC were previously known as Wellington Town FC
Nickname: 'The Bucks'
Ground: The New Bucks Head Stadium, Watling Street, Wellington, Telford TF1 2TU
Record Attendance: 13,000 (1935)

Pitch Size: 110 × 74 yards
Colours: White shirts with Black shorts
Telehone Nº: (01952) 640064
Fax Number: (01952) 640021
Ground Capacity: 5,780
Seating Capacity: 2,280
Web site: www.telfordutd.co.uk

GENERAL INFORMATION

Car Parking: At the ground
Coach Parking: At the ground
Nearest Railway Station: Wellington
Nearest Bus Station: Wellington
Club Shop: At the ground
Opening Times: Tuesdays and Thursdays 4.00pm to 6.00pm and Saturday Matchdays from 1.30pm
Telephone Nº: None

GROUND INFORMATION

Away Supporters' Entrances & Sections:
Frank Nagington Stand on the rare occasions when segregation is used

ADMISSION INFO (2012/2013 PRICES)

Adult Standing: £13.00
Adult Seating: £14.00
Under-14s Standing: £1.00 (with a paying adult)
Under-14s Seating: £2.00 (with a paying adult)
Under-18s Standing: £5.00
Under-18s Seating: £6.00
Senior Citizen Standing: £10.00
Senior Citizen Seating: £11.00

DISABLED INFORMATION

Wheelchairs: Accommodated at both ends of the ground
Helpers: Admitted
Prices: Normal prices apply
Disabled Toilets: Available
Contact: (01952) 640064   (Bookings are not necessary)

Travelling Supporters' Information:
Routes: Exit the M54 at Junction 6 and take the A518. Go straight on at the first roundabout, take the second exit at the next roundabout then turn left at the following roundabout. Follow the road round to the right then turn left into the car park.

ALFRETON TOWN FC

Founded: 1959
Former Names: None
Nickname: 'Reds'
Ground: The Impact Arena, North Street, Alfreton, Derbyshire DE55 7FZ
Record Attendance: 5,023 vs Matlock Town (1960)
Pitch Size: 110 × 75 yards

Colours: Red shirts and shorts
Telephone Nº: (0115) 939-2090
Fax Number: (0115) 949-1846
Ground Capacity: 4,238
Seating Capacity: 1,600
Web site: www.alfretontownfc.com

GENERAL INFORMATION

Car Parking: At the ground
Coach Parking: Available close to the ground
Nearest Railway Station: Alfreton (½ mile)
Nearest Bus Station: Alfreton (5 minutes walk)
Club Shop: At the ground
Opening Times: Matchdays only
Telephone Nº: (01773) 830277

GROUND INFORMATION

Away Supporters' Entrances & Sections:
Segregation is usual so please check prior to the game

ADMISSION INFO (2012/2013 PRICES)

Adult Standing: £18.00
Adult Seating: £18.00
Senior Citizen Standing: £12.00
Senior Citizen Seating: £12.00
Under-16s Standing: £3.00 (with a paying adult)
Under-16s Seating: £3.00 (with a paying adult)

DISABLED INFORMATION

Wheelchairs: Accommodated in dedicated areas of the ground
Helpers: Admitted
Prices: Please phone the club for information
Disabled Toilets: Available
Contact: (01773) 830277 (Bookings are not necessary)

Travelling Supporters' Information:
Routes: Exit the M1 at Junction 28 and take the A38 signposted for Derby. After 2 miles take the sliproad onto the B600 then go right at the main road towards the town centre. After ½ mile turn left down North Street and the ground is on the right after 200 yards.

BARROW FC

Founded: 1901
Former Names: None
Nickname: 'Bluebirds'
Ground: Furness Building Society Stadium, Barrow-in-Furness, Cumbria   LA14 5UW
Record Attendance: 16,874 (1954)
Pitch Size: 110 × 75 yards

Colours: White shirts with Blue shorts
Telephone Nº: (01229) 823061
Fax Number: (01229) 823061
Ground Capacity: 4,057
Seating Capacity: 928
Web site: www.barrowafc.com
E-mail: office@barrowafc.com

GENERAL INFORMATION

Car Parking: Street Parking, Popular Side Car Park and Soccer Bar Car Park
Coach Parking: Adjacent to the ground
Nearest Railway Station: Barrow Central (½ mile)
Nearest Bus Station: ½ mile
Club Shop: At the ground
Opening Times: Monday to Friday 9.00am – 3.30pm and Saturdays 10.00am – 2.00pm
Telephone Nº: (01229) 823061

GROUND INFORMATION

Away Supporters' Entrances & Sections:
West Terrace (not covered)

ADMISSION INFO (2012/2013 PRICES)

Adult Standing: £14.00
Adult Seating: £15.00
Concessionary Standing: £11.00
Concessionary Seating: £12.00
Under-16s Standing/Seating: £6.00
Under-7s Standing/Seating: £3.00

DISABLED INFORMATION

Wheelchairs: 6 spaces available in the Disabled Area
Helpers: Admitted
Prices: Normal prices apply
Disabled Toilets: Available
Contact: (01229) 823061   (Bookings are not necessary)

Travelling Supporters' Information:
Routes: Exit the M6 at Junction 36 and take the A590 through Ulverston. Using the bypass, follow signs for Barrow. After approximately 5 miles, turn left into Wilkie Road and the ground is on the right.

BRAINTREE TOWN FC

Founded: 1898
Former Names: Manor Works FC, Crittall Athletic FC, Braintree & Crittall Athletic FC and Braintree FC
Nickname: 'The Iron'
Ground: Amlin Stadium, Clockhouse Way, Braintree, Essex   CM7 3RD
Record Attendance: 4,000 (May 1952)
Pitch Size: 111 × 78 yards

Ground Capacity: 4,148
Seating Capacity: 553
Colours: Orange shirts and socks with Blue shorts
Telephone Nº: (01376) 345617
Fax Number: (01376) 330976
Correspondence Address: Tom Woodley, 19A Bailey Bridge Road, Braintree   CM7 5TT
Contact Telephone Nº: (01376) 326234
Web site: www.braintreetownfc.org.uk

GENERAL INFORMATION

Car Parking: At the ground
Coach Parking: At the ground
Nearest Railway Station: Braintree (1 mile)
Nearest Bus Station: Braintree
Club Shop: At the ground
Opening Times: Matchdays only
Telephone Nº: (01376) 345617

GROUND INFORMATION

Away Supporters' Entrances & Sections:
Gates 7-8

ADMISSION INFO (2012/2013 PRICES)

Adult Standing: £14.00 – £16.00
Adult Seating: £15.00 – £17.00
Senior Citizen Standing: £10.00
Under-16s Standing: £5.00
Under-11s Standing: £3.00
Note: Prices vary depending on the category of the game

DISABLED INFORMATION

Wheelchairs: Accommodated – 6 spaces available in the Main Stand
Helpers: Admitted
Prices: Normal prices apply
Disabled Toilets: Available
Contact: (01376) 345617

Travelling Supporters' Information:
Routes: Exit the A120 Braintree Bypass at the McDonald's roundabout and follow Cressing Road northwards. The floodlights at the ground are visible on the left ½ mile into town. Turn left into Clockhouse Way then left again for the ground.

CAMBRIDGE UNITED FC

Founded: 1912
Former Name: Abbey United FC (1912-1951)
Nickname: 'U's' 'United'
Ground: The R Costings Abbey Stadium,
Newmarket Road, Cambridge   CB5 8LN
Ground Capacity: 8,339
Seating Capacity: 4,376
Pitch Size: 110 × 74 yards

Record Attendance: 14,000 (1st May 1970)
Colours: Amber shirts, Black shorts
Telephone Nº: (01223) 566500
Ticket Office: (01223) 566500
Fax Number: (01223) 729220
Web Site: www.cambridgeunited.com
E-mail: info@cambridge-united.co.uk

GENERAL INFORMATION

Car Parking: Street parking only
Coach Parking: Coldhams Road
Nearest Railway Station: Cambridge (2 miles)
Nearest Bus Station: Cambridge City Centre
Club Shop: At the ground
Opening Times: Monday to Friday 9.30am to 4.00pm and
Matchdays 11.00am to kick-off
Telephone Nº: (01223) 566500

GROUND INFORMATION

Away Supporters' Entrances & Sections:
Coldham Common turnstiles 20-22 – Habbin Terrace (South)
and South Stand (Seating) turnstiles 23-26

ADMISSION INFO (2012/2013 PRICES)

Adult Standing: £15.00
Adult Seating: £17.00 – £19.00
Under-16s Standing: £5.00
Under-16s Seating: £6.00 – £9.00
Junior U's Standing: £2.00
Junior U's Seating: £3.00
Concessionary Standing: £10.00
Concessionary Seating: £11.00 – £12.00

DISABLED INFORMATION

Wheelchairs: 19 spaces in total for Home fans in the
disabled sections, in front of Main Stand and in the North
Terrace. 16 spaces for Away fans in the South Stand.
Helpers: One helper admitted per disabled fan
Prices: £10.00 – £12.00 for the disabled. Free for helpers
Disabled Toilets: At the rear of the disabled section
Contact: (01223) 566500   (Early booking strongly advised)

Travelling Supporters' Information: From the North: Take the A14 from Huntingdon, then turn east along the A14 dual
carriageway. Exit the A14 at the 4th junction (to the east of Cambridge), up the slip road signposted Stow-cum-Quy then turn
right onto the A1303, returning westwards towards Cambridge. Go straight on at the first roundabout passing the Airport on
the left then straight on at two sets of traffic lights. Go straight on at the next roundabout and the ground is on the left after 700
yards; From the South: Exit the M11 at Junction 14 and turn east along the A14 dual carriageway. Then as from the North.
Bus Services: Services from the Railway Station to the City Centre and Nº 3 from the City Centre to the Ground.

DARTFORD FC

Founded: 1888
Former Names: None
Nickname: 'The Darts'
Ground: Princes Park Stadium, Grassbanks, Darenth Road, Dartford DA1 1RT
Record Attendance: 4,097 (11th November 2006)
Pitch Size: 110 × 71 yards

Colours: White Shirts with Black Shorts
Telephone Nº: (01322) 299990
Fax Number: (01322) 299996
Ground Capacity: 4,097
Seating Capacity: 640
Web Site: www.dartfordfc.co.uk
E-mail: info@dartfordfc.co.uk

GENERAL INFORMATION
Car Parking: At the ground
Coach Parking: At the ground
Nearest Railway Station: Dartford (½ mile)
Nearest Bus Station: Dartford (½ mile) & Bluewater (2 miles)
Club Shop: At the ground
Opening Times: Matchdays only – 1.00pm to 6.00pm.
Telephone Nº: (01322) 299990

ADMISSION INFO (2012/2013 PRICES)
Adult Standing: £15.00
Adult Seating: £15.00
Senior Citizen/Concessionary Standing: £8.00
Senior Citizen/Concessionary Seating: £8.00
Under-12s Standing: £3.00
Under-12s Seating: £3.00

DISABLED INFORMATION
Wheelchairs: Accommodated
Helpers: Admitted
Prices: Concessionary prices for the disabled and helpers
Disabled Toilets: Available
Contact: (01322) 299991 (Bookings are not necessary)

Travelling Supporters' Information:
Routes: From M25 Clockwise: Exit the M25 at Junction 1B. At the roundabout, take the 3rd exit onto Princes Road (A225) then the second exit at the next roundabout.* Continue downhill to the traffic lights (with the ground on the left), turn left into Darenth Road then take the 2nd left for the Car Park; From M25 Anti-clockwise: Exit the M25 at Junction 2 and follow the A225 to the roundabout. Take the first exit at this roundabout then the 2nd exit at the next roundabout. Then as from * above.

EBBSFLEET UNITED FC

Founded: 1946
Former Names: Gravesend & Northfleet United FC, Gravesend United FC and Northfleet United FC
Nickname: 'The Fleet'
Ground: Stonebridge Road, Northfleet, Gravesend, Kent DA11 9GN
Record Attendance: 12,063 (1963)
Pitch Size: 112 × 72 yards

Colours: Reds shirts with White shorts
Telephone Nº: (01474) 533796
Fax Number: (01474) 324754
Ground Capacity: 5,258
Seating Capacity: 1,220
Web site: www.ebbsfleetunited.co.uk
E-mail: info@eufc.co.uk

GENERAL INFORMATION
Car Parking: Ebbsfleet International Car Park C (when available) and also street parking
Coach Parking: At the ground
Nearest Railway Station: Northfleet (5 minutes walk)
Nearest Bus Station: Bus Stop outside the ground
Club Shop: At the ground
Opening Times: Matchdays only
Telephone Nº: (01474) 533796

GROUND INFORMATION
Away Supporters' Entrances & Sections:
Only some games are segregated – contact club for details

ADMISSION INFO (2012/2013 PRICES)
Adult Standing: £15.00
Adult Seating: £17.00
Concessionary Standing: £10.00
Concessionary Seating: £12.00
Under-12s Standing/Seating: £5.00
Note: Family Tickets are also available

DISABLED INFORMATION
Wheelchairs: 6 spaces are available in the Disabled Area in front of the Main Stand
Helpers: Admitted free of charge
Prices: Please phone the club for information
Disabled Toilets: Available in the Main Stand
Contact: (01474) 533796 (Bookings are necessary)

Travelling Supporters' Information:
Routes: Take the A2 to the Northfleet/Southfleet exit and follow signs for Northfleet (B262). Go straight on at the first roundabout then take the 2nd exit at the 2nd roundabout into Thames Way and follow the football signs for the ground.

FOREST GREEN ROVERS FC |

Founded: 1889
Former Names: Stroud FC
Nickname: 'The Rovers'
Ground: The New Lawn, Smiths Way, Forest Green, Nailsworth, Gloucestershire, GL6 0FG
Record Attendance: 4,836 (3rd January 2009)
Pitch Size: 110 × 70 yards

Colours: Black and White striped shirts, Black shorts
Telephone Nº: (01453) 834860
Fax Number: (01453) 835291
Ground Capacity: 5,147
Seating Capacity: 2,500
Web site: www.forestgreenroversfc.com
E-mail: reception@forestgreenroversfc.com

GENERAL INFORMATION
Car Parking: At the ground
Coach Parking: At the ground
Nearest Railway Station: Stroud (4 miles)
Nearest Bus Station: Nailsworth
Club Shop: At the ground
Opening Times: Matchdays only
Telephone Nº: (01453) 834860

GROUND INFORMATION
Away Supporters' Entrances & Sections:
EESI Stand

ADMISSION INFO (2012/2013 PRICES)
Adult Standing: £14.00
Adult Seating: £16.00
Senior Citizen Standing: £10.00
Senior Citizen Seating: £12.00
Child Standing: £4.00
Child Seating: £5.00

DISABLED INFORMATION
Wheelchairs: Accommodated in the Main Stand
Helpers: Admitted
Prices: Normal prices for the disabled. Free for helpers
Disabled Toilets: Yes
Contact: (01453) 834860 (Enquiries necessary at least 72 hours in advance)

Travelling Supporters' Information:
Routes: The ground is located 4 miles south of Stroud on the A46 to Bath. Upon entering Nailsworth, turn into Spring Hill at the mini-roundabout and the ground is approximately ½ mile up the hill on the left.

GATESHEAD FC

Founded: 1930   (Reformed in 1977)
Former Names: Gateshead United FC
Nickname: 'Tynesiders'
Ground: International Stadium, Neilson Road, Gateshead   NE10 0EF
Record Attendance: 11,750 (1995)
Pitch Size: 110 × 70 yards

Colours: White shirts with Black shorts
Telephone Nº: (0191) 478-3883
Fax Number: (0191) 440-0404
Ground Capacity: 11,750
Seating Capacity: 11,750
Web site: www.gateshead-fc.com
E-mail: info@gateshead-fc.com

GENERAL INFORMATION
Car Parking: At the stadium
Coach Parking: At the stadium
Nearest Railway Station: Gateshead Stadium Metro (½ mile); Newcastle (British Rail) 1½ miles
Nearest Bus Station: Heworth Interchange (½ mile)
Club Shop: At the stadium
Opening Times: Matchdays only
Telephone Nº: (0191) 478-3883

GROUND INFORMATION
Away Supporters' Entrances & Sections:
Tyne & Wear County Stand North End or the East Stand

ADMISSION INFO (2012/2013 PRICES)
Adult Seating: £14.00
Senior Citizen/Concessionary Seating: £9.00
Under-16s Seating: £2.00

DISABLED INFORMATION
Wheelchairs: 5 spaces available each for home and away fans by the trackside – Level access with automatic doors
Helpers: Admitted
Prices: Normal prices for the disabled. Helpers are admitted free of charge.
Disabled Toilets: Available in the Reception Area and on the 1st floor concourse – accessible by lift.
Contact: (0191) 478-3883   (Bookings are necessary)

Travelling Supporters' Information:
Routes: From the South: Take the A1(M) to Washington Services and fork right onto the A194(M) signposted Tyne Tunnel. At the next roundabout, turn left onto the A184 signposted for Gateshead. The Stadium is on the right after 3 miles.

GRIMSBY TOWN FC

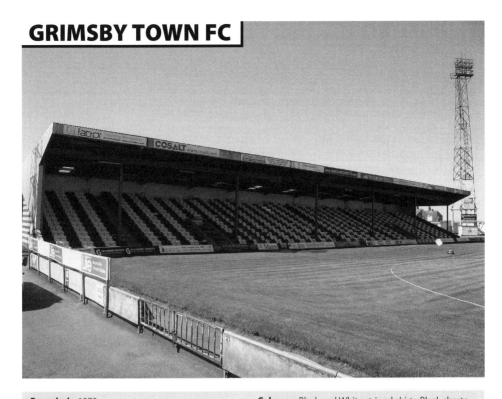

Founded: 1878
Former Names: Grimsby Pelham FC (1879)
Nickname: 'Mariners'
Ground: Blundell Park, Cleethorpes   DN35 7PY
Ground Capacity: 8,974 (All seats)
Record Attendance: 31,651 (20th February 1937)
Pitch Size: 111 × 74 yards

Colours: Black and White striped shirts, Black shorts
Telephone N°: (01472) 605050
Ticket Office: (01472) 605050
Fax Number: (01472) 693665
Web Site: www.grimsby-townfc.co.uk
E-mail: info@gtfc.co.uk

GENERAL INFORMATION

Car Parking: Street parking
Coach Parking: Harrington Street – near the ground
Nearest Railway Station: Cleethorpes (1½ miles)
Nearest Bus Station: Brighowgate, Grimsby (4 miles)
Club Shop: At the ground
Opening Times: Monday – Friday 9.00am to 5.00pm;
Matchday Saturdays 9.00am to kick-off
Telephone N°: (01472) 605050

GROUND INFORMATION

Away Supporters' Entrances & Sections:
Harrington Street turnstiles 15-18 and Constitution Avenue
turnstiles 5-14

ADMISSION INFO (2012/2013 PRICES)

Adult Seating: £18.00 (Away fans £18.00)
Senior Citizen Seating: £12.00
Young Adults Seating (Ages 15–18): £12.00
Child Seating: £8.00 (Under-15s)
Note: Tickets are cheaper if purchased before the matchday

DISABLED INFORMATION

Wheelchairs: 50 spaces in total for Home and Away fans in
the disabled section, in front of the Main Stand
Helpers: Helpers are admitted
Prices: £18.00 for the disabled. Free of charge for helpers
Disabled Toilets: Available in disabled section
Commentaries are available in disabled section
Contact: (01472) 605050 (Bookings are necessary)

Travelling Supporters' Information:
Routes: From All Parts except Lincolnshire and East Anglia: Take the M180 to the A180 and follow signs for Grimsby/
Cleethorpes. The A180 ends at a roundabout (the 3rd in short distance after crossing docks), take the 2nd exit from the roundabout
over the Railway flyover into Cleethorpes Road (A1098) and continue into Grimsby Road. After the second stretch of dual
carriageway, the ground is ½ mile on the left; From Lincolnshire: Take the A46 or A16 and follow Cleethorpes signs along
(A1098) Weelsby Road for 2 miles. Take the 1st exit at the roundabout at the end of Clee Road into Grimsby Road. The ground is
1¾ miles on the right.

HEREFORD UNITED FC

Founded: 1924	**Colours**: White shirts with Black shorts
Former Names: None	**Telephone N°**: 0844 276-1939
Nickname: 'United' 'The Bulls'	**Fax Number**: 0844 276-1982
Ground: Edgar Street, Hereford HR4 9JU	**Ground Capacity**: 5,710
Record Attendance: 18,114 (4th January 1958)	**Seating Capacity**: 3,390
Pitch Size: 110 × 70 yards	**Web site**: www.herefordunited.co.uk
	E-mail: club@herefordunited.co.uk

GENERAL INFORMATION

Car Parking: Merton Meadow Car Park (Near the ground)
Coach Parking: Merton Meadow Car Park
Nearest Railway Station: Hereford (½ mile)
Nearest Bus Station: Commercial Road, Hereford
Club Shop: At the ground
Opening Times: Weekdays 9.00am to 4.00pm and
Matchdays 12.00pm to 3.00pm
Telephone N°: 0844 276-1939

GROUND INFORMATION

Away Supporters' Entrances & Sections:
Blackfriars Street and Edgar Street for the Cargill Community
Stand and Blackfriars Street Temporary Stand (overflow)

ADMISSION INFO (2012/2013 PRICES)

Adult Standing: £16.00
Adult Seating: £18.00
Ages 11-14 Standing: £5.00
Ages 11-14 Seating: £7.00
Under-11s Standing: £3.00
Under-11s Seating: £3.00
Concessionary Standing: £12.00
Concessionary Seating: £15.00

DISABLED INFORMATION

Wheelchairs: 7 spaces in total for Home and Away fans in
the disabled section, MandMDirect.com Stand
Helpers: One helper admitted per disabled person
Prices: £12.00 for the disabled. Free of charge for helpers
Disabled Toilets: Available
Contact: 0844 276-1939 (Bookings are necessary)

Travelling Supporters' Information:
Routes: From the North: Follow A49 Hereford signs straight into Edgar Street; From the East: Take the A465 or A438 into Hereford Town Centre, then follow signs for Leominster (A49) into Edgar Street; From the South: Take the A49 or A45 into the Town Centre (then as East); From the West: Take the A438 into the Town Centre (then as East).

HYDE FC

Founded: 1919
Former Names: Hyde FC (1885-1917) and Hyde United FC (1917-2010)
Nickname: 'Tigers'
Ground: Tameside Stadium, Ewen Fields, Walker Lane, Hyde, Cheshire   SK14 5PL
Record Attendance: 9,500 (1952)
Pitch Size: 114 × 70 yards

Colours: White shirts with Navy Blue shorts
Telephone Nº: 0871 200-2116 (Matchdays) or 07778 792502 (Secretary)
Fax Number: 0871 200-2118 (Ground); (01270) 212473 (Secretary)
Ground Capacity: 4,250
Seating Capacity: 550
Web site: www.hydefc.co.uk
E-mail: secretary@hydefc.co.uk

GENERAL INFORMATION
Car Parking: 150 spaces available at the ground
Coach Parking: At the ground
Nearest Railway Station: Newton (¼ mile)
Nearest Bus Station: Hyde
Club Shop: At the ground
Opening Times: Matchdays only
Telephone Nº: 0871 200-2116

GROUND INFORMATION
Away Supporters' Entrances & Sections:
No usual segregation although it is used as required

ADMISSION INFO (2012/2013 PRICES)
Adult Standing: £14.00
Adult Seating: £16.00
Child Standing: £4.00
Child Seating: £6.00
Senior Citizen Standing: £7.00
Senior Citizen Seating: £9.00

DISABLED INFORMATION
Wheelchairs: Accommodated in the disabled area
Helpers: Please phone the club for information
Prices: Please phone the club for information
Disabled Toilets: Yes
Contact: (01270) 212473 (Bookings are not necessary)

Travelling Supporters' Information:
Routes: Exit the M60 at Junction 24 and then exit the M67 at Junction 3 for Hyde. Turn right at the top of the slip road, left at the lights (Morrisons on the left). Turn right at the next set of lights into Lumn Road then turn left at the Give Way sign into Walker Lane. Take the 2nd Car Park entrance near the Leisure Pool and follow the road round for the Stadium.

KIDDERMINSTER HARRIERS FC

Founded: 1886
Nickname: 'Harriers'
Ground: Aggborough, Hoo Road, Kidderminster, Worcestershire   DY10 1NB
Ground Capacity: 6,444
Seating Capacity: 3,143
Record Attendance: 9,155 (1948)

Pitch Size: 110 × 72 yards
Colours: Red shirts and shorts
Telephone Nº: (01562) 823931
Fax Number: (01562) 827329
Web Site: www.harriers.co.uk
E-mail: info@harriers.co.uk

GENERAL INFORMATION
Car Parking: At the ground
Coach Parking: As directed
Nearest Railway Station: Kidderminster
Nearest Bus Station: Kidderminster Town Centre
Club Shop: At the ground
Opening Times: Weekdays and First Team Matchdays 9.00am to 5.00pm
Telephone Nº: (01562) 823931

GROUND INFORMATION
Away Supporters' Entrances & Sections:
John Smiths Stand Entrance D and South Terrace Entrance E

ADMISSION INFO (2012/2013 PRICES)
Adult Standing: £14.00
Adult Seating: £17.00
Senior Citizen Standing: £8.00
Senior Citizen Seating: £11.00
Under-16s Standing: £5.00
Under-16s Seating: £8.00
Note: Under-8s are admitted free with a paying adult

DISABLED INFORMATION
Wheelchairs: Home fans accommodated at the front of the Main Stand, Away fans in front of the John Smiths Stand
Helpers: Admitted
Prices: £10.00 for each disabled fan plus one helper
Disabled Toilets: Available by the disabled area
Contact: (01562) 823931   (Bookings are not necessary)

Travelling Supporters' Information:
Routes: Exit the M5 at Junction 3 and follow the A456 to Kidderminster. The ground is situated close by the Severn Valley Railway Station so follow the brown Steam Train signs and turn into Hoo Road about 200 yards downhill of the station. Follow the road along for ¼ mile and the ground is on the left.

LINCOLN CITY FC

Founded: 1884
Nickname: 'Red Imps'
Ground: Sincil Bank Stadium, Lincoln   LN5 8LD
Ground Capacity: 10,120 (All seats)
Record Attendance: 23,196 (15th November 1967)
Pitch Size: 110 × 72 yards

Colours: Red and White striped shirts, Black shorts
Telephone Nº: (01522) 880011
Ticket Office: (01522) 880011
Fax Number: (01522) 880020
Web Site: www.redimps.com
E-mail: lcfc@redimps.com

GENERAL INFORMATION

Car Parking: Stacey West Car Park (limited parking for £5.00 per car).
Coach Parking: Please contact the club for details.
Nearest Railway Station: Lincoln Central
Club Shop: At the ground
Opening Times: Weekdays 9.00am to 5.00pm and Saturday Matchdays 10.00am to 5.00pm
Telephone Nº: (01522) 880011

GROUND INFORMATION

Away Supporters' Entrances & Sections:
Lincolnshire Co-operative Stand (seated) – Turnstiles 19-23

ADMISSION INFO (2011/2012 PRICES)

Adult Seating: £14.00 – £18.00
Child Seating: £6.00 – £7.00
Concessionary Seating: £10.00 – £13.00
Note: Prices vary depending on the category of the game and area of the ground and discounts are available for advance ticket purchases

DISABLED INFORMATION

Wheelchairs: Limited number of spaces available in the disabled section, adjacent to turnstile 23
Helpers: One helper admitted per disabled person
Prices: Applications for disabled passes must be made to the club. Wheelchair-bound disabled are charged concessionary prices. Helpers are admitted free if the disabled fan has a medium/high level disability allowance
Disabled Toilets: Adjacent to disabled area
Contact: (01522) 880011   (Bookings are necessary)

Travelling Supporters' Information:
Routes: From the East: Take the A46 or A158 into the City Centre following Newark (A46) signs into the High Street and take next left (Scorer Street and Cross Street) for the ground; From the North and West: Take the A15 or A57 into the City Centre, then as from the East; From the South: Take the A1 then A46 for the City Centre, then into the High Street, parking on the South Common or in the Stadium via South Park Avenue, turn down by the Fire Station.

LUTON TOWN FC

Founded: 1885
Former Names: The club was formed by the amalgamation of Wanderers FC and Excelsior FC
Nickname: 'Hatters'
Ground: Kenilworth Road Stadium, 1 Maple Road, Luton LU4 8AW
Ground Capacity: 10,226 (All seats)
Record Attendance: 30,069 (4th March 1959)

Pitch Size: 110 × 72 yards
Colours: Orange shirts with Blue shorts
Telephone N⁰: (01582) 411622
Ticket Office: (01582) 416976
Fax Number: (01582) 405070
Web Site: www.lutontown.co.uk
E-mail: info@lutontown.co.uk

GENERAL INFORMATION
Car Parking: Street parking
Coach Parking: Luton Bus Station
Nearest Railway Station: Luton (1 mile)
Nearest Bus Station: Bute Street, Luton
Club Shop: Kenilworth Road Forecourt
Opening Times: 10.00am to 4.00pm
Telephone N⁰: (01582) 411622

GROUND INFORMATION
Away Supporters' Entrances & Sections:
Oak Road for the Oak Stand

ADMISSION INFO (2012/2013 PRICES)
Adult Seating: £15.00 – £18.00
Under-10s Seating: £5.00
Under-17s Seating: £8.00
Under-22s Seating: £13.00
Senior Citizen Seating: £10.00 – £13.00
Note: Tickets are cheaper if bought prior to the matchday

DISABLED INFORMATION
Wheelchairs: 32 spaces in total for Home and Away fans in the disabled section, Kenilworth Road End and Main Stand
Helpers: One helper admitted per disabled person
Prices: £15.00 for the disabled. Free of charge for helpers
Disabled Toilets: Available adjacent to disabled area Commentaries are available for the blind
Contact: (01582) 416976 (Bookings are necessary)

Travelling Supporters' Information:
Routes: From the North and West: Exit the M1 at Junction 11 and follow signs for Luton (A505) into Dunstable Road. Follow the one-way system and turn right back towards Dunstable, take the second left into Ash Road for the ground; From the South and East: Exit the M1 at Junction 10 (or A6/A612) into Luton Town Centre and follow signs into Dunstable Road. After the railway bridge, take the sixth turning on the left into Ash Road for the ground.

MACCLESFIELD TOWN FC

Founded: 1874
Former Names: Macclesfield FC
Nickname: 'The Silkmen'
Ground: Moss Rose Ground, London Road, Macclesfield, Cheshire   SK11 7SP
Ground Capacity: 6,052
Seating Capacity: 2,485
Record Attendance: 10,041 (1948)

Pitch Size: 110 × 72 yards
Colours: Blue shirts, White shorts and Blue socks
Telephone Nº: (01625) 264686
Ticket Office: (01625) 264686
Fax Number: (01625) 264692
Web Site: www.mtfc.co.uk
E-mail: office@mtfc.co.uk

GENERAL INFORMATION

Car Parking: Ample parking available near the ground
Coach Parking: Near the ground
Nearest Railway Station: Macclesfield (1 mile)
Nearest Bus Station: Macclesfield
Club Shop: At the ground
Opening Times: Weekdays and matchdays 9.00am to 5.00pm
Telephone Nº: (01625) 264686

GROUND INFORMATION

Away Supporters' Entrances & Sections:
Silkman Terrace and the left side of the McAlpine Stand

ADMISSION INFO (2012/2013 PRICES)

Adult Standing: £14.00
Adult Seating: £18.00
Concessions Standing: £10.00
Concessions Seating: £14.00
Under-12s Standing: £3.00
Under-12s Seating: £3.00
Ages 12-15 Standing: £5.00
Ages 12-15 Seating: £5.00

DISABLED INFORMATION

Wheelchairs: 45 spaces in front of the Estate Road Stand
Helpers: One helper admitted per disabled fan
Prices: Concessionary prices for the disabled. Helpers are admitted free of charge
Disabled Toilets: 3 available
Contact: (01625) 264686   (Bookings are necessary)

Travelling Supporters' Information:
Routes: From the North: Exit the M6 at Junction 19 to Knutsford, follow the A537 to Macclesfield. Follow signs for the Town Centre, then for the A523 to Leek. The ground is 1 mile out of the Town Centre on the right; From the South: Exit M6 at Junction 17 for Sandbach and follow the A534 to Congleton. Then take the A536 to Macclesfield. After passing The Rising Sun on the left, ¼ mile further on turn right after the Texaco Garage (Moss Lane). Following this lane will bring you back to the ground.

MANSFIELD TOWN FC

Founded: 1897
Former Name: Mansfield Wesleyans FC (1897-1905)
Nickname: 'Stags'
Ground: Field Mill Ground, Quarry Lane, Mansfield, Nottinghamshire NG18 5DA
Ground Capacity: 10,000 (All seats)
Record Attendance: 24,467 (10th January 1953)
Pitch Size: 114 × 70 yards

Colours: Amber shirts with Royal Blue piping, Royal Blue shorts with Amber flash
Telephone Nº: (01623) 482483
Ticket Office: (01623) 482483
Fax Number: (01623) 482495
Web Site: www.mansfieldtown.net
E-mail: info@mansfieldtown.net

GENERAL INFORMATION
Car Parking: Large car park at the ground (£2.50)
Coach Parking: Adjacent to the ground
Nearest Railway Station: Mansfield (5 minutes walk)
Nearest Bus Station: Mansfield
Club Shop: In the South Stand of the Stadium
Opening Times: Weekdays 9.00am – 5.00pm and Matchdays 10.00am – 3.00pm
Telephone Nº: (0870) 756-3160

GROUND INFORMATION
Away Supporters' Entrances & Sections:
North Stand turnstiles for North Stand seating

ADMISSION INFO (2012/2013 PRICES)
Adult Seating: £15.00 – £18.00
Senior Citizen Seating: £12.00
Junior Seating: £7.00 – £9.00
Under-7s Seating: £2.00

DISABLED INFORMATION
Wheelchairs: 90 spaces available in total in the disabled sections in the North Stand, Quarry Street Stand & West Stand
Helpers: Admitted
Prices: £8.00 for the disabled. Helpers £15.00
Disabled Toilets: Available in the North Stand, West Stand and Quarry Lane Stand
Contact: (0870) 756-3160 (Please buy tickets in advance)

Travelling Supporters' Information:
Routes: From the North: Exit the M1 at Junction 29 and take the A617 to Mansfield. After 6¼ miles turn right at the Leisure Centre into Rosemary Street. Carry on to Quarry Lane and turn right; From the South and West: Exit the M1 at Junction 28 and take the A38 to Mansfield. After 6½ miles turn right at the crossroads into Belvedere Street then turn right after ¼ mile into Quarry Lane; From the East: Take the A617 to Rainworth, turn left at the crossroads after 3 miles into Windsor Road and turn right at the end into Nottingham Road, then left into Quarry Lane.

NEWPORT COUNTY AFC

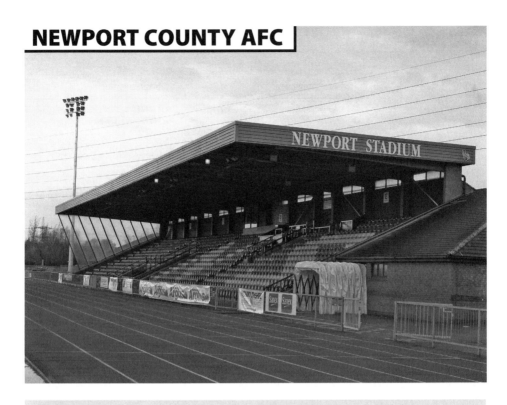

Founded: 1989
Former Names: Newport AFC
Nickname: 'The Exiles'
Ground: Newport Stadium, Stadium Way, Newport International Sports Village, Newport NP19 4PT
Record Attendance: 4,616 (11th November 2006)
Pitch Size: 112 × 72 yards

Colours: Amber shirts with Black shorts
Telephone N°: (01633) 662262
Fax Number: (01633) 666107
Ground Capacity: 4,300
Seating Capacity: 1,236
Web site: www.newport-county.co.uk
E-mail: office@newport-county.co.uk

GENERAL INFORMATION
Car Parking: Space for 500 cars at the ground
Coach Parking: At the ground
Nearest Railway Station: Newport
Nearest Bus Station: Newport
Club Shop: At the ground
Opening Times: Matchdays only
Telephone N°: (01633) 662262

GROUND INFORMATION
Away Supporters' Entrances & Sections:
No segregation unless specifically required by the Police

ADMISSION INFO (2012/2013 PRICES)
Adult Standing: £17.00
Adult Seating: £17.00
Senior Citizen Standing: £11.00
Senior Citizen Seating: £13.00
Full-time Student Standing: £11.00
Full-time Student Seating: £13.00
Under-16s Standing: £5.00
Under-16s Seating: £8.00
Note: Under-6s are admitted free of charge

DISABLED INFORMATION
Wheelchairs: Accommodated
Helpers: Admitted
Prices: Normal prices for the disabled. Free for helpers
Disabled Toilets: Yes
Contact: (01633) 662262   (Bookings are not necessary)

Travelling Supporters' Information:
Routes: Exit the M4 at Junction 24 and take the A48 exit at the roundabout, signposted 'Newport Int. Sports Village'. Go straight on at the first two roundabouts then bear left at the 3rd roundabout. Carry straight on over the next two roundabouts, then turn left before the Carcraft site. Take the 1st turning on the left into the Stadium car park.

NUNEATON TOWN FC

Founded: 1937 (Reformed 2008)
Former Names: Nuneaton Borough FC
Nickname: 'Boro'
Ground: Triton Showers Community Arena,
Liberty Way, Attleborough Fields Industrial Estate,
Nuneaton   CV11 6RR
Record Attendance: 3,111 (2nd May 2009)
Pitch Size: 109 × 74 yards

Colours: Blue shirts and white shorts
Telephone Nº: (024) 7638-5738
Daytime Phone Nº: (024) 7638-5738
Fax Number: (024) 7637-2995
Ground Capacity: 4,500
Seating Capacity: 500
Web site: www.nuneatontownfc.com
E-mail: admin@nuneatontownfc.com

GENERAL INFORMATION

Car Parking: On-site car park plus various other parking spaces available on the nearby Industrial Estate
Coach Parking: At the ground
Nearest Railway Station: Nuneaton (2 miles)
Nearest Bus Station: Nuneaton (2 miles)
Club Shop: Yes – The Boro Shop
Opening Times: By appointment and also on matchdays
Telephone Nº: (024) 7638-5738

GROUND INFORMATION

Away Supporters' Entrances & Sections:
No usual segregation

ADMISSION INFO (2012/2013 PRICES)

Adult Standing: £12.00 – £14.00
Adult Seating: £14.00 – £16.00
Concessionary Standing: £8.00 – £10.00
Concessionary Seating: £10.00 – £12.00
Under-16s Standing/Seating: £5.00
Under-12s Standing/Seating: £2.00
Note: Prices vary depending on the category of the game.

DISABLED INFORMATION

Wheelchairs: Accommodated
Helpers: Please phone the club for information
Prices: Please phone the club for information
Disabled Toilets: Available
Contact: (024) 7638-5738   (Bookings are necessary)

Travelling Supporters' Information:
Routes: From the South, West and North-West: Exit the M6 at Junction 3 and follow the A444 into Nuneaton. At the Coton Arches roundabout turn right into Avenue Road which is the A4254 signposted for Hinckley. Continue along the A4254 following the road into Garrett Street then Eastboro Way then turn left into Townsend Drive. Follow the road round before turning left into Liberty Way for the ground; From the North: Exit the M1 at Junction 21 and follow the M69. Exit the M69 at Junction 1 and take the 4th exit at the roundabout onto the A5 (Tamworth, Nuneaton). At Longshoot Junction, turn left onto the A47, continue to the roundabout and take the 1st exit onto A4254 Eastborough Way. Turn right at the next roundabout into Townsend Drive then immediately right again for Liberty Way.

SOUTHPORT FC

Founded: 1881
Former Names: Southport Vulcan FC, Southport Central FC
Nickname: 'The Sandgrounders'
Ground: Haig Avenue, Southport, Merseyside, PR8 6JZ
Record Attendance: 20,010 (1932)
Pitch Size: 110 × 77 yards

Colours: Yellow shirts and shorts
Telephone Nº: (01704) 533422
Fax Number: (01704) 533455
Ground Capacity: 6,008
Seating Capacity: 1,600
Web site: www.southportfc.net

GENERAL INFORMATION
Car Parking: Street parking
Coach Parking: Adjacent to the ground
Nearest Railway Station: Southport (1½ miles)
Nearest Bus Station: Southport Town Centre
Club Shop: At the ground
Opening Times: Matchdays from 1.30pm (from 6.30pm on evening matchdays)
Telephone Nº: (01704) 533422

GROUND INFORMATION
Away Supporters' Entrances & Sections:
Blowick End entrances

ADMISSION INFO (2012/2013 PRICES)
Adult Standing: £12.50
Adult Seating: £14.00
Senior Citizen Standing: £9.00
Senior Citizen Seating: £10.00
Under-19s Standing/Seating: £5.00
Note: Children aged 11 and under are admitted free of charge when accompanied by a paying adult.

DISABLED INFORMATION
Wheelchairs: Accommodated in front of the Grandstand
Helpers: Admitted
Prices: Concessionary prices charged for the disabled. Helpers are admitted free of charge
Disabled Toilets: Available at the Blowick End of the Grandstand
Contact: (01704) 533422 (Bookings are not necessary)

Travelling Supporters' Information:
Routes: Exit the M58 at Junction 3 and take the A570 to Southport. At the major roundabout (McDonalds/Tesco) go straight on into Scarisbrick New Road, pass over the brook and turn right into Haig Avenue at the traffic lights. The ground is then on the right-hand side.

STOCKPORT COUNTY FC

Founded: 1883
Former Names: Heaton Norris Rovers FC
Nickname: 'Hatters' 'County'
Ground: Edgeley Park, Hardcastle Road, Edgeley, Stockport SK3 9DD
Ground Capacity: 10,641 (All seats)
Record Attendance: 27,833 (11th February 1950)
Pitch Size: 111 × 72 yards

Colours: Blue shirts and shorts
Telephone Nº: (0161) 286-8903
Ticket Office: 0845 688-5799
Fax Number: (0161) 429-7392
Web Site: www.stockportcounty.com
E-mail: fans@stockportcounty.com

GENERAL INFORMATION

Car Parking: Booth Street (nearby) £4.00
Coach Parking: Booth Street (£20.00)
Nearest Railway Station: Stockport (5 minutes walk)
Nearest Bus Station: Mersey Square (10 minutes walk)
Club Shop: At the ground
Opening Times: Monday, Wednesday and Friday from 9.30am – 5.00pm. Open until 7.30pm on matchdays during the week and also on Saturday matchdays 10.00am – 2.45pm then for 30 minutes after the game.
Telephone Nº: (0161) 286-8888

GROUND INFORMATION

Away Supporters' Entrances & Sections:
Railway End turnstiles for Railway End or turnstiles for Popular Side depending on the opponents

ADMISSION INFO (2012/2013 PRICES)

Adult Seating: £16.00 – £18.00
Under-22s Seating: £11.00
Under-17s Seating: £3.00
Under-7s Seating: Free of charge
Senior Citizen Seating: £11.00

DISABLED INFORMATION

Wheelchairs: 16 spaces in total. 10 in the Hardcastle Road Stand, 6 in the Cheadle Stand
Helpers: One helper admitted per disabled fan
Prices: £11.00 for the disabled. Helpers free of charge
Disabled Toilets: Yes
Contact: 0845 688-5799 (Bookings are necessary)

Travelling Supporters' Information:
Routes: From the North, South and West: Exit the M63 at Junction 11 and join the A560, following signs for Cheadle. After ¼ mile turn right into Edgeley Road and after 1 mile turn right into Caroline Street for the ground; From the East: Take the A6 or A560 into Stockport Town Centre and turn left into Greek Street. Take the 2nd exit into Mercian Way (from the roundabout) then turn left into Caroline Street – the ground is straight ahead.

TAMWORTH FC

Founded: 1933
Former Names: None
Nickname: 'The Lambs'
Ground: The Lamb Ground, Kettlebrook, Tamworth, B77 1AA
Record Attendance: 4,920 (3rd April 1948)
Pitch Size: 110 × 73 yards

Colours: Red shirts with Black shorts
Telephone N°: (01827) 65798
Fax Number: (01827) 62236
Ground Capacity: 4,118
Seating Capacity: 520
Web site: www.thelambs.co.uk

GENERAL INFORMATION

Car Parking: 200 spaces available at the ground – £2.00 per car, £5.00 for per minibus or £10.00 per coach
Coach Parking: At the ground
Nearest Railway Station: Tamworth (½ mile)
Nearest Bus Station: Tamworth (½ mile)
Club Shop: At the ground
Opening Times: Weekdays from 10.00am to 4.00pm and also on Matchdays
Telephone N°: (01827) 65798

GROUND INFORMATION

Away Supporters' Entrances & Sections:
Gates 1 and 2 for Terracing, Gate 2A for seating

ADMISSION INFO (2012/2013 PRICES)

Adult Standing: £12.00 – £14.00
Adult Seating: £14.00 – £16.00
Under-16s Standing: £3.00 – £4.00 (Under-6s free)
Under-16s Seating: £5.00 – £6.00
Senior Citizen Standing: £7.00 – £9.00
Senior Citizen Seating: £9.00 – £11.00
Note: Prices vary depending on the category of the game.

DISABLED INFORMATION

Wheelchairs: Accommodated
Helpers: Admitted
Prices: Normal prices apply for Wheelchair disabled. Helpers are charged concessionary rates
Disabled Toilets: Yes
Contact: (01827) 65798 (Bookings are advisable)

Travelling Supporters' Information:
Routes: Exit the M42 at Junction 10 and take the A5/A51 to the town centre following signs for Town Centre/Snowdome. The follow signs for Kettlebrook and the ground is in Kettlebrook Road, 50 yards from the traffic island by the Railway Viaduct and the Snowdome. The ground is signposted from all major roads.

WOKING FC

Founded: 1889
Former Names: None
Nickname: 'Cardinals'
Ground: Kingfield Stadium, Kingfield, Woking, Surrey   GU22 9AA
Record Attendance: 6,000 (1997)
Pitch Size: 109 × 76 yards

Colours: Shirts are Red & White halves, Black shorts
Telephone Nº: (01483) 772470
Daytime Phone Nº: (01483) 772470
Fax Number: (01483) 888423
Ground Capacity: 6,161
Seating Capacity: 2,511
Web site: www.wokingfc.co.uk
E-mail: admin@wokingfc.co.uk

GENERAL INFORMATION

Car Parking: Limited parking at the ground
Coach Parking: At or opposite the ground
Nearest Railway Station: Woking (1 mile)
Nearest Bus Station: Woking
Club Shop: At the ground
Opening Times: Weekdays and Matchdays
Telephone Nº: (01483) 772470

GROUND INFORMATION

Away Supporters' Entrances & Sections:
Kingfield Road entrance for the Tennis Club terrace

ADMISSION INFO (2012/2013 PRICES)

Adult Standing: £15.00
Adult Seating: £15.00
Under-16s/Student Standing: £5.00
Under-16s/Student Seating: £5.00
Senior Citizen Standing: £10.00
Senior Citizen Seating: £10.00

DISABLED INFORMATION

Wheelchairs: 8 spaces in the Leslie Gosden Stand and 8 spaces in front of the Family Stand
Helpers: Admitted
Prices: One wheelchair and helper for £8.00
Disabled Toilets: Yes – in the Leslie Gosden Stand and Family Stand area
Contact: (01483) 772470   (Bookings are necessary)

Travelling Supporters' Information:
Routes: Exit the M25 at Junction 10 and follow the A3 towards Guildford. Leave at the next junction onto the B2215 through Ripley and join the A247 to Woking. Alternatively, exit the M25 at Junction 11 and follow the A320 to Woking Town Centre. The ground is on the outskirts of Woking – follow signs on the A320 and A247.

WREXHAM FC

Founded: 1872
Nickname: 'Red Dragons'
Ground: Racecourse Ground, Mold Road, Wrexham, North Wales LL11 2AH
Ground Capacity: 10,500 (all seats)
Record Attendance: 34,445 (26th January 1957)
Pitch Size: 111 × 71 yards

Colours: Red shirts with White shorts
Telephone Nº: (01978) 262129
Fax Number: (01978) 357821
Web Site: www.wrexhamafc.co.uk
E-mail: info@wrexhamfc.tv

GENERAL INFORMATION

Car Parking: Town car parks are nearby and also Glyndwr University (Mold End)
Coach Parking: By Police direction
Nearest Railway Station: Wrexham General (adjacent)
Nearest Bus Station: Wrexham (King Street)
Club Shop: At the ground in the Yale Stand
Opening Times: Monday to Saturday 9.00am to 5.00pm
Telephone Nº: (01978) 262129

GROUND INFORMATION

Away Supporters' Entrances & Sections:
Turnstiles 1-4 for the Yale Stand

ADMISSION INFO (2012/2013 PRICES)

Adult Seating: £14.00 – £18.00
Under-16s Seating: £5.00
Under-11s Seating: £2.00
Concessionary Seating: £10.00 – £12.00
Over-80s Seating: £5.00
Note: Family tickets are also available

DISABLED INFORMATION

Wheelchairs: 35 spaces in the Mold Road Stand
Helpers: One helper admitted per wheelchair
Prices: Normal prices for the disabled. Free for helpers
Disabled Toilets: Available in the disabled section
Contact: (01978) 262129 (Bookings are preferred)

Travelling Supporters' Information:
Routes: From the North and West: Take the A483 and the Wrexham bypass to the junction with the A541. Branch left at the roundabout and follow Wrexham signs into Mold Road; From the East: Take the A525 or A534 into Wrexham then follow the A541 signs into Mold Road; From the South: Take the the M6, then the M54 and follow the A5 and A483 to the Wrexham bypass and the junction with the A541. Branch right at the roundabout and follow signs for the Town Centre.

THE FOOTBALL CONFERENCE BLUE SQUARE NORTH

Address

Third Floor, Wellington House,
31-34 Waterloo Street, Birmingham   B2 5TJ

Phone (0121) 214-1950

Web site   www.footballconference.co.uk

Clubs for the 2012/2013 Season

ALTRINCHAM FC

Founded: 1891
Former Names: Broadheath FC
Nickname: 'The Robins'
Ground: Moss Lane, Altrincham   WA15 8AP
Record Attendance: 10,275 (February 1925)
Pitch Size: 110 × 72 yards
Web site: www.altrinchamfc.com

Colours: Red and White striped shirts, Black shorts
Telephone Nº: (0161) 928-1045
Daytime Phone Nº: (0161) 928-1045
Fax Number: (0161) 926-9934
Ground Capacity: 6,085
Seating Capacity: 1,154
E-mail: office@altrinchamfootballclub.co.uk

GENERAL INFORMATION
Car Parking: Limited street parking
Coach Parking: By Police Direction
Nearest Railway Station: Altrincham (15 minutes walk)
Nearest Bus Station: Altrincham
Club Shop: Inside the ground
Opening Times: Matchdays only. Opens one hour prior to the start of the game.
Telephone Nº: (0161) 928-1045

GROUND INFORMATION
Away Supporters' Entrances & Sections:
Hale End turnstiles and accommodation

ADMISSION INFO (2012/2013 PRICES)
Adult Standing: £13.00
Adult Seating: £15.00
Concessionary Standing: £8.00
Concessionary Seating: £9.00
Ages 12-16 years Standing/Seating: £5.00
Under-12s Standing/Seating: £2.00

DISABLED INFORMATION
Wheelchairs: 3 spaces are available each for home and away fans adjacent to the Away dugout
Helpers: Admitted
Prices: Free for the disabled. £13.00 for helpers
Disabled Toilets: Yes
Contact: (0161) 928-1045   (Bookings are necessary)

Travelling Supporters' Information:
Routes: Exit the M56 at either Junction 6 or 7 and follow the signs for Altrincham FC.

BISHOP'S STORTFORD FC

Founded: 1874
Former Names: None
Nickname: 'Blues' 'Bishops'
Ground: Woodside Park, Dunmow Road, Bishop's Stortford CM23 5RG
Record Attendance: 3,555 (2000)
Pitch Size: 110 × 70 yards

Colours: Blue and White shirts with Blue shorts
Telephone Nº: (01279) 306456
Fax Number: (01279) 715621
Ground Capacity: 4,000
Seating Capacity: 500
Web site: www.bsfc.co.uk

GENERAL INFORMATION
Car Parking: 500 spaces available at the ground
Coach Parking: At the ground
Nearest Railway Station: Bishop's Stortford
Nearest Bus Station: Bishop's Stortford
Club Shop: At the ground
Opening Times: Matchdays only 1.30pm to 5.00pm
Telephone Nº: (01279) 306456

GROUND INFORMATION
Away Supporters' Entrances & Sections:
No usual segregation

ADMISSION INFO (2012/2013 PRICES)
Adult Standing/Seating: £12.00
Concessionary Standing/Seating: £7.00
Student Standing/Seating: £6.00
Under-16s Standing/Seating: £5.00
Note: Under-12s are admitted free of charge when accompanied by a paying adult.

DISABLED INFORMATION
Wheelchairs: Accommodated in the disabled section
Helpers: Admitted
Prices: Free of charge for the disabled and helpers
Disabled Toilets: Yes
Contact: (01279) 306456 (Bookings are not necessary)

Travelling Supporters' Information:
Routes: Exit the M11 at junction 8 and take the A1250 towards Bishop Stortford. Turn left at the first roundabout and the ground is first right opposite the Golf Club (the entrance is between Industrial Units).

BOSTON UNITED FC

Founded: 1933
Former Names: Boston Town FC & Boston Swifts FC
Nickname: 'The Pilgrims'
Ground: Jakeman's Stadium, York Street, Boston, PE21 6JN
Ground Capacity: 6,613 **Seating Capacity**: 2,000
Pitch Size: 112 × 72 yards

Record Attendance: 10,086 (1955)
Colours: Amber and Black shirts, Black shorts
Telephone Nº: (01205) 364406 (Office)
Matchday Info: (01205) 364406 or 07860 663299
Fax Number: (01205) 354063
Web Site: www.bufc.co.uk
E-mail: admin@bufc.co.uk

GENERAL INFORMATION
Car Parking: Permit holders only
Coach Parking: Available near to the ground
Nearest Railway Station: Boston (1 mile)
Nearest Bus Station: Boston Coach Station (¼ mile)
Club Shop: In the car park at the ground
Opening Times: Weekdays from 9.00am to 5.00pm and Saturday Matchdays from 11.00am to 5.00pm
Telephone Nº: (01205) 364406

GROUND INFORMATION
Away Supporters' Entrances & Sections:
York Street Entrances 3 & 4 (subject to a move to the Jakemans Stand if so advised by the police)

ADMISSION INFO (2012/2013 PRICES)
Adult Standing: £12.00
Adult Seating: £14.00
Child Standing: £4.00
Child Seating: £5.00
Senior Citizen Standing: £9.00
Senior Citizen Seating: £10.00

DISABLED INFORMATION
Wheelchairs: 7 spaces available for home fans, 4 spaces for away fans below the Main Stand at the Town End
Helpers: One helper admitted per disabled fan
Prices: £12.00 for the disabled. Free of charge for helpers
Disabled Toilets: Available in the Town End Terrace
Contact: (01205) 364406 (Bookings are necessary)

Travelling Supporters' Information:
From the North: Take the A17 from Sleaford, bear right after the railway crossing to the traffic lights over the bridge. Go forward through the traffic lights into York Street for the ground; From the South: Take the A16 from Spalding and turn right at the traffic lights over the bridge. Go forward through the next traffic lights into York Street for the ground.

BRACKLEY TOWN FC |

Founded: 1890
Former Names: None
Nickname: 'Saints'
Ground: St. James Park, Churchill Way, Brackley, NN13 7EJ
Record Attendance: 980 (2009/10 season)

Colours: Red and White striped shirts with Red shorts
Telephone Nº: (01280) 704077
Ground Capacity: 3,500
Seating Capacity: 300
Web Site: www.brackleytownfc.com

GENERAL INFORMATION

Car Parking: At the ground (£2.00 charge per car)
Coach Parking: At the ground
Nearest Railway Station: King's Sutton (6¾ miles)
Club Shop: At the ground
Opening Times: Matchdays and by appointment only
Telephone Nº: (01280) 704077

GROUND INFORMATION

Away Supporters' Entrances & Sections:
No usual segregation

ADMISSION INFO (2012/2013 PRICES)

Adult Standing: £10.00
Adult Seating: £10.00
Senior Citizen/Student Standing: £5.00
Senior Citizen/Student Seating: £5.00
Under-16s Standing: £2.00
Under-16s Seating: £2.00

DISABLED INFORMATION

Wheelchairs: Accommodated
Helpers: Admitted
Prices: Normal prices apply for the disabled and helpers
Disabled Toilets: Available
Contact: (01280) 704077 (Stephen Toghill – bookings are necessary)

Travelling Supporters' Information:
Routes: From the West: Take the A422 to Brackley and take the first exit at the roundabout with the junction of the A43, heading north into Oxford Road.* Go straight on at the next roundabout and continue into Bridge Street before turning right into Churchill Way. The ground is located at the end of the road; From the South: Take the A43 northwards to Brackley. Take the second exit at the roundabout with the junction of the A422 and head into Oxford Road. Then as from * above; From the North-East: Take the A43 to Brackley. Upon reaching Brackley, take the 1st exit at the 1st roundabout, the 2nd exit at the next roundabout then the 3rd exit at the following roundabout into Oxford Road. Then as from * above.

BRADFORD PARK AVENUE FC

Founded: 1907   (Re-formed in 1988)
Former Names: None
Nickname: 'Avenue'
Ground: Horsfall Stadium, Cemetery Road, Bradford, BD6 2NG
Record Attendance: 2,100 (2003)
Pitch Size: 112 × 71 yards

Colours: Green & White striped shirts, White shorts
Telephone Nº: (01274) 604578 (Ground)
Office Number: (01274) 660066
Ground Capacity: 3,000
Seating Capacity: 1,247
Web site: www.bpafc.com

GENERAL INFORMATION
Car Parking: Street parking and some spaces at the ground
Coach Parking: At the ground
Nearest Railway Station: Bradford Interchange (3 miles)
Nearest Bus Station: Bradford Interchange (3 miles)
Club Shop: At the ground
Opening Times: Matchdays only
Telephone Nº: –

GROUND INFORMATION
Away Supporters' Entrances & Sections:
Segregation only used when required

ADMISSION INFO (2012/2013 PRICES)
Adult Standing/Seating: £10.00
Senior Citizen Standing/Seating: £6.00
Student Standing/Seating: £6.00
Under-16s Standing/Seating: £2.00
Armed Forces Standing/Seating: £2.00 (warrant card must be shown)

DISABLED INFORMATION
Wheelchairs: Accommodated in front of the Stand
Helpers: Please phone the club for information
Prices: Please phone the club for information
Disabled Toilets: Available
Contact: –   (Bookings are not necessary)

Travelling Supporters' Information:
Routes: Exit the M62 at Junction 26 and take the M606 to its end. At the roundabout go along the A6036 (signposted Halifax) and pass Odsal Stadium on the left. At the roundabout by Odsal take the 3rd exit (still A6036 Halifax). After just under 1 mile, turn left at the King's Head pub into Cemetery Road. The ground is 150 yards on the left.

CHESTER FC

Founded: 1885	**Record Attendance**: 5,987 (17th April 2004)
Former Names: Chester FC and Chester City FC	**Colours**: Blue and White striped shirts, Black shorts
Nickname: 'City'	**Ticket Office**: (01244) 371376
Ground: Exacta Stadium, Bumpers Lane, Chester,	**Fax Number**: (01244) 390265
CH1 4LT **Ground Telephone Nº**: (01244) 371376	**Ground Capacity**: 5,556 **Seating Capacity**: 4,170
Pitch Size: 116 × 75 yards	**Web site**: www.chesterfc.com

GENERAL INFORMATION

Car Parking: Ample spaces available at the ground (£1.00)
Coach Parking: Available at the ground
Nearest Railway Station: Chester (2 miles)
Nearest Bus Station: Chester (1½ miles)
Club Shop: At the ground
Opening Times: Weekdays & matchdays 10.00am–4.00pm
Telephone Nº: (01244) 371376

GROUND INFORMATION

Away Supporters' Entrances & Sections:
South Stand for covered seating and also part of the West Stand

ADMISSION INFO (2012/2013 PRICES)

Adult Standing: £12.00
Adult Seating: £14.00
Senior Citizen Standing: £9.00
Senior Citizen Seating: £10.00
Under-18s Seating/Standing: £5.00
Under-16s Seating/Standing: £3.00 (Under-5s free)

DISABLED INFORMATION

Wheelchairs: 32 spaces for wheelchairs (with 40 helpers) in the West Stand and East Stand
Helpers: One helper admitted per disabled person
Prices: Concessionary prices for the disabled. Free for helpers
Disabled Toilets: Available in West and East Stands
Contact: (01244) 371376 (Bookings are necessary)

Travelling Supporters' Information:
Routes: From the North: Take the M56, A41 or A56 into the Town Centre and then follow Queensferry (A548) signs into Sealand Road. Turn left at the traffic lights by 'Tesco' into Bumpers Lane – the ground is ½ mile at the end of the road; From the East: Take the A54 or A51 into the Town Centre (then as North); From the South: Take the A41 or A483 into Town Centre (then as North); From the West: Take the A55, A494 or A548 and follow Queensferry signs towards Birkenhead (A494) and after 1¼ miles bear left onto the A548 (then as North); From the M6/M56 (Avoiding Town Centre): Take the M56 to Junction 16 (signposted Queensferry), turn left at the roundabout onto A5117, signposted Wales. At the next roundabout turn left onto the A5480 (signposted Chester) and after approximately 3 miles take the 3rd exit from the roundabout (signposted Sealand Road Industrial Parks). Go straight across 2 sets of traffic lights into Bumpers Lane. The ground is ½ mile on the right.

COLWYN BAY FC

Founded: 1885
Former Names: None
Nickname: 'Bay' 'Seagulls'
Ground: Llanelian Road, Old Colwyn, Colwyn Bay, LL29 8UN
Record Attendance: 2,500

Colours: Sky Blue shirts and shorts
Telephone Nº: (01492) 514680
Ground Capacity: 2,500
Seating Capacity: 500
Web site: www.colwynbayfc.co.uk

GENERAL INFORMATION
Car Parking: At the ground
Coach Parking: At the ground
Nearest Railway Station: Colwyn Bay (1 mile)
Nearest Bus Station: Colwyn Bay
Club Shop: At the ground
Opening Times: Matchdays only
Telephone Nº: (01422) 341222

GROUND INFORMATION
Away Supporters' Entrances & Sections:
No usual segregation

ADMISSION INFO (2012/2013 PRICES)
Adult Standing/Seating: £9.00
Concessionary Standing/Seating: £5.00
Student Standing/Seating: £5.00
Under-14s Standing/Seating: £2.00

DISABLED INFORMATION
Wheelchairs: Accommodated in Covered Terrace
Helpers: Admitted
Prices: Please phone the club for information
Disabled Toilets: Available in the Social Club
Contact: (01492) 514581   (Bookings are not necessary)

Travelling Supporters' Information:
Routes: From Queensferry: Take the A55 and when the expressway is reached take Junction 22 (signposted Old Colwyn). Turn left at the bottom of the slip road then straight on at the mini-roundabout into Llanelian Road. The ground is ½ mile on the right.

CORBY TOWN FC

Photograph courtesy of Chris Rivett, Final Third Sports Media

Founded: 1948
Former Names: None
Nickname: 'The Steelmen'
Ground: Steel Park, Jimmy Kane Way, Rockingham Road, Corby   NN17 2FB
Record Attendance: 2,240 vs Watford (1986/87)
Pitch Size: 109 × 70 yards

Colours: White shirts with Black shorts
Telephone N°: (01536) 406640
Fax Number: (0116) 237-6162
Ground Capacity: 3,893
Seating Capacity: 577
Web site: www.corbytownfc.co.uk
E-mail: info@corbytownfc.co.uk

GENERAL INFORMATION
Car Parking: Spaces for 190 cars at the ground
Coach Parking: Spaces for 3 coaches at the ground
Nearest Railway Station: Corby (2 miles)
Nearest Bus Station: Corby Town Centre
Club Shop: At the ground
Opening Times: Matchdays only – 1 hour before kick-off
Telephone N°: (01536) 406640

GROUND INFORMATION
Away Supporters' Entrances & Sections:
No usual segregation

ADMISSION INFO (2012/2013 PRICES)
Adult Standing/Seating: £10.00
Senior Citizen Standing/Seating: £7.00
Under-16s Standing/Seating: Free of charge

DISABLED INFORMATION
Wheelchairs: Accommodated
Helpers: Admitted
Prices: Normal prices apply for disabled fans. Helpers are admitted free of charge
Disabled Toilets: Available
Contact: (01536) 406640   (Bookings are not necessary)

Travelling Supporters' Information:
Routes: From the North & East: Exit the A1(M) at junction 17 and take the A605 to Oundle then the A427 to Little Weldon. At the roundabout take the A6116 towards Rockingham and the ground is adjacent to Rockingham Castle near the junction with the A6003; From the South: Take the A14 to the junction with the A6116 and continue to the junction with the A6003 at Rockingham Castle; From the West: Take the A14 or A427 to the A6003 then continue north towards Rockingham to the junction with the A6116 where the ground is on the left.

DROYLSDEN FC

Founded: 1892
Former Names: None
Nickname: 'The Bloods'
Ground: Butchers Arms, Market Street, Droylsden, Manchester   M43 7AY
Record Attendance: 5,400 (1973)
Pitch Size: 110 × 70 yards

Colours: Red shirts with Red shorts
Telephone Nº: (0161) 370-1426
Daytime Phone Nº: (0161) 370-1426
Fax Number: (0161) 370-8341
Ground Capacity: 3,500
Seating Capacity: 500
Web site: www.droylsdenfc.com

GENERAL INFORMATION
Car Parking: Street parking only
Coach Parking: At the ground
Nearest Railway Station: Manchester Piccadilly
Nearest Bus Station: Ashton
Club Shop: At the ground
Opening Times: Matchdays only
Telephone Nº: (0161) 370-1426

GROUND INFORMATION
Away Supporters' Entrances & Sections:
No usual segregation

ADMISSION INFO (2012/2013 PRICES)
Adult Standing: £10.00
Adult Seating: £10.00
Concessionary Standing: £6.00
Concessionary Seating: £6.00
Under-16s Standing: £2.00
Under-16s Seating: £2.00

DISABLED INFORMATION
Wheelchairs: Accommodated beside the Stand
Helpers: Yes
Prices: Normal prices apply for the disabled and helpers
Disabled Toilets: Available
Contact: (0161) 370-1426   (Bookings are not necessary)

Travelling Supporters' Information:
Routes: Take the Manchester Outer Ring Road M60 and exit at Junction 23. Join the A635 towards Manchester and after the retail park on the left, take the centre lane, then turn right at the traffic lights onto the A662 signposted for Droylsden. At the next traffic lights, turn right onto Market Street and after 150 yards go straight on at the traffic lights. The entrance to the ground is 75 yards on the left.

FC HALIFAX TOWN

Founded: 1911 (Re-formed 2008)
Former Names: Halifax Town FC
Nickname: 'The Shaymen'
Ground: The Shay Stadium, Shay Syke, Halifax, HX1 2YT
Ground Capacity: 10,568
Seating Capacity: 5,285

Record Attendance: 4,023 (1st January 2011)
Pitch Size: 112 × 73 yards
Colours: Blue shirts and shorts
Telephone Nº: (01422) 341222
Fax Number: (01422) 349487
Web Site: www.halifaxafc.co.uk
E-mail: secretary@halifaxafc.co.uk

GENERAL INFORMATION

Car Parking: Adjacent to the East Stand and also Shaw Hill Car Park (Nearby)
Coach Parking: By arrangement with the Club Secretary
Nearest Railway Station: Halifax (10 minutes walk)
Nearest Bus Station: Halifax (15 minutes walk)
Club Shop: At the ground in the East Stand
Opening Times: Please phone for details
Telephone Nº: (01422) 341222 (to change during the 2011/12 season)

GROUND INFORMATION

Away Supporters' Entrances & Sections:
Skircoat Stand (Seating only)

ADMISSION INFO (2012/2013 PRICES)

Adult Standing/Seating: £13.00
Under-16s Standing/Seating: £7.50
Senior Citizen Standing/Seating: £10.00
Under-12s Standing/Seating: £5.00
Under-7s Standing/Seating: £2.00

DISABLED INFORMATION

Wheelchairs: 33 spaces available in total in disabled sections in the East Stand and South Stand
Helpers: One admitted free with each paying disabled fan
Prices: Free of charge for the disabled and helpers
Disabled Toilets: Available in the East and South Stands
Contact: (01422) 434212 (Bookings are not necessary)

Travelling Supporters' Information:
Routes: From the North: Take the A629 to Halifax Town Centre. Take the 2nd exit at the roundabout into Broad Street and follow signs for Huddersfield (A629) into Skircoat Road; From the South, East and West: Exit the M62 at Junction 24 and follow Halifax (A629) signs for the Town Centre into Skircoat Road then Shaw Hill for ground.

GAINSBOROUGH TRINITY FC

Founded: 1873
Former Names: None
Nickname: 'The Blues'
Ground: Northolme, Gainsborough, Lincolnshire, DN21 2QW
Record Attendance: 9,760 (1948)
Pitch Size: 111 × 71 yards

Colours: Blue shirts and shorts
Telephone Nº: (01427) 613295
Clubhouse Phone Nº: (01427) 613688
Fax Number: (01427) 613295
Ground Capacity: 4,340
Seating Capacity: 504
Web site: www.gainsboroughtrinity.com

GENERAL INFORMATION

Car Parking: Street parking and also in a Local Authority Car Park 150 yards from the ground towards the Town Centre
Coach Parking: Available by prior arrangement
Nearest Railway Station: Lea Road (2 miles)
Nearest Bus Station: Heaton Street (1 mile)
Club Shop: At the ground
Opening Times: Matchdays only
Telephone Nº: (01427) 611612

GROUND INFORMATION

Away Supporters' Entrances & Sections:
No usual segregation

ADMISSION INFO (2012/2013 PRICES)

Adult Standing: £10.00
Adult Seating: £11.00
Concessionary Standing: £6.00
Concessionary Seating: £7.00
Under-16s Standing/Seating: £2.00
Under-11s Standing/Seating: £1.00

DISABLED INFORMATION

Wheelchairs: Accommodated
Helpers: Please phone the club for information
Prices: Normal prices for the disabled. Free for helpers
Disabled Toilets: Available in new block adjacent to the Main Stand
Contact: (01427) 613295 (Bookings are not necessary)

Travelling Supporters' Information:
Routes: From the North, South and West: Exit the A1 at Blyth services taking the 1st left through to Bawtry. In Bawtry, turn right at the traffic lights onto the A631 straight through to Gainsborough (approx. 11 miles). Go over the bridge to the second set of traffic lights and turn left onto the A159 (Scunthorpe Road). Follow the main road past Tesco on the right through the traffic lights. The ground is situated on right approximately a third of a mile north of the Town Centre; From the East: Take the A631 into Gainsborough and turn right onto the A159. Then as above.

GLOUCESTER CITY FC

Gloucester City are groundsharing with Cheltenham Town FC for the 2012/2013 season.

Founded: 1889 (**Re-formed**: 1980)
Forner Names: Gloucester YMCA
Nickname: 'The Tigers'
Ground: Abbey Business Stadium, Whaddon Road, Cheltenham, Gloucestershire GL52 5NA
Ground Capacity: 7,136
Seating Capacity: 4,054

Record Attendance: 8,326 (1956)
Pitch Size: 110 × 72 yards
Colours: Yellow and Black Striped shirts, Black shorts
Telephone N⁰: 07813 931781
Web Site: www.gloucestercityafc.com
E-mail: contact@gloucestercityafc.com

GENERAL INFORMATION

Car Parking: Very limited parking available at the ground. A Park & Ride scheme runs from Cheltenham Race Course and other car parks are available in Cheltenham Town Centre
Coach Parking: At the ground
Nearest Railway Station: Cheltenham Spa (2½ miles)
Nearest Bus Station: Cheltenham Royal Well
Club Shop: At the ground
Opening Times: Matchdays only

GROUND INFORMATION

Away Supporters' Entrances & Sections:
No usual segregation

ADMISSION INFO (2012/2013 PRICES)

Adult Standing: £12.00
Adult Seating: £12.00
Child Standing: £6.00
Child Seating: £6.00
Concessionary Standing: £6.00
Concessionary Seating: £6.00

DISABLED INFORMATION

Wheelchairs: Accommodated in front of the Stagecoach West Stand (use main entrance) and in the In 2 Print Stand
Helpers: Admitted free of charge
Prices: Normal prices apply for disabled fans
Disabled Toilets: Available in the In 2 Print Stand, adjacent to the Stagecoach West Stand and in the Social Club
Contact: 07813 931781

Travelling Supporters' Information:
Routes: The ground is situated to the North-East of Cheltenham, 1 mile from the Town Centre off the B4632 (Prestbury Road) – Whaddon Road is to the East of the B4632 just North of Pittville Circus. Road signs in the vicinity indicate 'Whaddon Road/ Cheltenham Town FC'.

GUISELEY AFC

Founded: 1909
Former Names: None
Nickname: 'The Lions'
Ground: Nethermoor, Otley Road, Guiseley, Leeds, LS20 8BT
Record Attendance: 2,486 (1989/90)
Pitch Size: 110 × 69 yards

Colours: White shirts with Navy Blue shorts
Telephone Nº: (01943) 873223
Social Club Phone Nº: (01943) 872872
Fax Number: (01943) 873223
Ground Capacity: 3,000
Seating Capacity: 300
Web site: www.guiseleyafc.co.uk
E-mail: admin@guiseleyafc.co.uk

GENERAL INFORMATION
Car Parking: At the ground and in Ings Crescent
Coach Parking: At the ground
Nearest Railway Station: Guiseley (5 minute walk)
Nearest Bus Station: Bus Stop outside the ground
Club Shop: At the ground
Opening Times: Matchdays only
Telephone Nº: (01943) 879236 (weekdays)
Postal Sales: Yes

GROUND INFORMATION
Away Supporters' Entrances & Sections:
No usual segregation

ADMISSION INFO (2012/2013 PRICES)
Adult Standing: £10.00
Adult Seating: £10.00
Under-12s Standing: £1.00
Under-12s Seating: £1.00
Concessionary Standing: £6.00
Concessionary Seating: £6.00

DISABLED INFORMATION
Wheelchairs: Accommodated by the Players' Entrance
Helpers: Admitted
Prices: Free for both disabled fans and helpers
Disabled Toilets: None
Contact: (01943) 879236 (Bookings are advisable)

Travelling Supporters' Information:
Routes: Exit the M62 at Junction 28 and take the Leeds Ring Road to the roundabout at the junction of the A65 at Horsforth. Turn left onto the A65 and pass through Rawdon to Guiseley keeping Morrison's supermarket on your left. Pass straight through the traffic lights with the Station pub or your right and the ground is on the right after ¼ mile, adjacent to the cricket field.

HARROGATE TOWN FC

Founded: 1919
Former Names: Harrogate FC and Harrogate Hotspurs FC
Nickname: 'Town'
Ground: CNG Stadium, Wetherby Road, Harrogate, HG2 7SA
Record Attendance: 4,280 (1950)
Pitch Size: 107 × 72 yards

Colours: Yellow and Black striped shirts, Black shorts
Telephone Nº: (01423) 880675 or 883671
Club Fax Number: (01423) 880675
Ground Capacity: 3,290
Seating Capacity: 502
Web site: www.harrogatetown.com
E-mail: enquiries@harrogatetown.com

GENERAL INFORMATION
Car Parking: Hospital Car Park adjacent
Coach Parking: At the ground
Nearest Railway Station: Harrogate (¾ mile)
Nearest Bus Station: Harrogate
Club Shop: At the ground
Opening Times: Monday to Friday 9.00am to 3.00pm and also on Matchdays
Telephone Nº: (01423) 885525

GROUND INFORMATION
Away Supporters' Entrances & Sections:
No usual segregation

ADMISSION INFO (2012/2013 PRICES)
Adult Standing: £12.00
Adult Seating: £12.00
Concessionary Standing: £7.00
Concessionary Seating: £7.00
Under-16s Standing: £3.00 (when with a paying adult)
Under-16s Seating: £3.00 (when with a paying adult)
Note: Under-5s are admitted free of charge

DISABLED INFORMATION
Wheelchairs: Accommodated at the front of the Main Stand
Helpers: One helper admitted for each disabled fan
Prices: Free of charge for each disabled fan and helper
Disabled Toilets: Available
Contact: (01423) 880675 (Bookings are necessary)

Travelling Supporters' Information:
Routes: From the South: Take the A61 from Leeds and turn right at the roundabout onto the ring road (signposted York). After about 1¼ miles turn left at the next roundabout onto A661 Wetherby Road. The ground is situated ¾ mile on the right; From the West: Take the A59 straight into Wetherby Road from Empress Roundabout and the ground is on the left; From the East & North: Exit the A1(M) at Junction 47, take the A59 to Harrogate then follow the Southern bypass to Wetherby Road for the A661 Roundabout. Turn right towards Harrogate Town Centre and the ground is on the right after ¾ mile.

HINCKLEY UNITED FC

Founded: 1889
Former Names: Formed when Hinckley Athletic FC merged with Hinckley Town FC in 1997 (previously Westfield Rovers FC)
Nickname: 'The Knitters'
Ground: The Greene King Stadium, De Montfort Park, Leicester Road, Hinckley   LE10 3DR
Record Attendance: 3,231 (1st July 2008)

Pitch Size: 110 × 72 yards
Colours: Red and Blue halved shirts with Blue shorts
Telephone Nº: (01455) 840088
Contact Number: (01455) 840088
Ground Capacity: 4,329
Seating Capacity: 630
Web site: www.hinckleyunitedfc.co.uk
E-mail: raybaggott@yahoo.co.uk

GENERAL INFORMATION
Car Parking: At the ground (£2.00 charge per car)
Coach Parking: At the ground (£10.00 charge per coach, £5.00 charge per minibus)
Nearest Railway Station: Hinckley (2 miles)
Nearest Bus Station: Hinckley
Club Shop: At the ground
Opening Times: Matchdays only
Telephone Nº: (01455) 840088

GROUND INFORMATION
Away Supporters' Entrances & Sections:
West Stand and Terrace if required (no usual segregation)

ADMISSION INFO (2012/2013 PRICES)
Adult Standing: £10.00
Adult Seating: £12.00
Under-16s Standing: £3.00 (Under-11s free of charge)
Under-16s Seating: £5.00
Senior Citizen Standing: £7.00
Senior Citizen Seating: £9.00

DISABLED INFORMATION
Wheelchairs: Accommodated
Helpers: Admitted
Prices: Normal prices apply
Disabled Toilets: Yes
Contact: (01455) 840088 (Bookings are not necessary)

Travelling Supporters' Information:
Routes: From the North-West: Take the A5 southbound and take the 1st exit at Dodwells roundabout onto the A47 towards Earl Shilton. Go straight on over 3 roundabouts then take the 3rd exit at the next roundabout onto the B4668. The entrance to the ground is on the right after 200 yards; From the South: Take the A5 northbound and upon reaching Dodwells roundabout take the 2nd exit onto the A47 towards East Shilton. Then as above; From the North-East: Take the M69, exit at Junction 2 and follow the B4669 towards Hinckley. After 2 miles (passing through 2 sets of traffic lights) bear right into Spa Lane then turn right at the next set of traffic lights onto the B4668 towards Earl Shilton. The Stadium is on the left after 1¾ miles.

HISTON FC

Founded: 1904
Former Names: Histon Institute FC
Nickname: 'The Stutes'
Ground: The Glass World Stadium, Bridge Road, Impington, Cambridge CB24 9PH
Record Attendance: 6,400 (1956)
Pitch Size: 110 × 75 yards

Colours: Red and Black striped shirts, Black shorts
Telephone Nº: (01223) 237373
Fax Number: (01223) 237495
Ground Capacity: 4,100
Seating Capacity: 1,626
Web site: www.histonfc.co.uk
E-mail: enquiries@histonfc.co.uk

GENERAL INFORMATION

Car Parking: Permit holders and disabled parking only at the ground. Check web site for details of fans parking
Coach Parking: For team coaches only
Nearest Railway Station: Cambridge (4 miles)
Nearest Bus Station: Cambridge (4 miles) (Use Citi Seven service for the ground)
Club Shop: At the ground
Opening Times: Three hours prior to kick-off for both Saturday and evening matches.
Telephone Nº: (01223) 237373

GROUND INFORMATION

Away Supporters' Entrances & Sections:
No usual segregation

ADMISSION INFO (2012/2013 PRICES)

Adult Standing: £10.00
Adult Seating: £10.00
Child Standing: £3.00
Child Seating: £3.00
Senior Citizen Standing: £6.00
Senior Citizen Seating: £6.00

DISABLED INFORMATION

Wheelchairs: 6 spaces available in the home section and 6 spaces available in the away section
Helpers: Admitted
Prices: Normal prices apply for the disabled. Free for helpers
Disabled Toilets: Available in both the home and away sections
Contact: Mac McDonald (Club safety officer) 07730 557021

Travelling Supporters' Information:
Routes: Exit the M11 at Junction 14 and follow the A14 eastwards. Take the first exit onto the B1049 (signposted Histon & Cottenham). Turn left at the traffic lights at the top of the slip road and pass the Holiday Inn on the right. Continue over the bridge and the entrance to the ground is on the right.

OXFORD CITY FC

Founded: 1882
Former Names: None
Nickname: 'City'
Ground: Court Place Farm, Marsh Lane, Marston, Oxford   OX3 0NQ
Record Attendance: 9,500 (1950)

Colours: Blue & White hooped shirts with Blue shorts
Telephone Nº: (01865) 744493
Ground Capacity: 3,000
Seating Capacity: 300
Web Site: www.oxfordcityfc.co.uk

GENERAL INFORMATION

Car Parking: At the ground
Coach Parking: At the ground
Nearest Railway Station: Oxford (3¾ miles)
Club Shop: At the ground
Opening Times: Matchdays only
Telephone Nº: (01865) 744493

GROUND INFORMATION

Away Supporters' Entrances & Sections:
No usual segregation

ADMISSION INFO (2012/2013 PRICES)

Adult Standing: £11.00
Adult Seating: £11.00
Concessionary Standing: £6.00
Concessionary Seating: £6.00
Under-16s Standing: Free of charge
Under-16s Seating: Free of charge

DISABLED INFORMATION

Wheelchairs: Accommodated
Helpers: Admitted
Prices: Normal prices apply for the disabled and helpers
Disabled Toilets: Available
Contact: (01865) 744493   (Bookings are not necessary)

Travelling Supporters' Information:
Routes: The stadium is located by the side of the A40 Northern Bypass Road next to the Marston flyover junction to the north east of Oxford. Exit the A40 at the Marston junction and head into Marsh Lane (B4150). Take the first turn on the left into the OXSRAD Complex then turn immediately left again to follow the approach road to the stadium in the far corner of the site.

SOLIHULL MOORS FC

Founded: 2007
Former Names: Formed by the merger of Solihull Borough FC and Moor Green FC in 2007
Nickname: 'The Moors'
Ground: Damson Park, Damson Parkway, Solihull, B91 2PP
Record Attendance: 2,000 (vs Birmingham City)
Pitch Size: 110 × 75 yards

Colours: White shirts with Black shorts
Telephone Nº: (0121) 705-6770
Fax Number: (0121) 711-4045
Ground Capacity: 3,050
Seating Capacity: 280
Web site: www.solihullmoorsfc.co.uk
E-mail: robin.lamb5@btinternet.com

GENERAL INFORMATION
Car Parking: At the ground
Coach Parking: At the ground
Nearest Railway Station: Birmingham International (2 miles)
Nearest Bus Station: Birmingham (5 miles)
Club Shop: At the ground
Opening Times: Matchdays only
Telephone Nº: (0121) 705-6770

GROUND INFORMATION
Away Supporters' Entrances & Sections:
No usual segregation

ADMISSION INFO (2012/2013 PRICES)
Adult Standing: £12.00
Adult Seating: £12.00
Senior Citizen/Junior Standing: £6.00
Senior Citizen/Junior Seating: £6.00
Note: Under-16s can purchase a season ticket for £30.00

DISABLED INFORMATION
Wheelchairs: Spaces for 3 wheelchairs are available
Helpers: Admitted
Prices: Normal prices apply
Disabled Toilets: Available
Contact: (0121) 705-6770

Travelling Supporters' Information:
Routes: Exit the M42 at Junction 6 and take the A45 for 2 miles towards Birmingham. Turn left at the traffic lights near the Posthouse Hotel into Damson Parkway (signposted for Landrover/Damsonwood). Continue to the roundabout and come back along the other carriageway to the ground which is situated on the left after about 150 yards.

STALYBRIDGE CELTIC FC

Founded: 1909
Former Names: None
Nickname: 'Celtic'
Ground: Bower Fold, Mottram Road, Stalybridge, Cheshire   SK15 2RT
Record Attendance: 9,753 (1922/23)
Pitch Size: 109 × 70 yards

Colours: Blue shirts, White shorts and Blue socks
Telephone Nº: (0161) 338-2828
Daytime Phone Nº: (0161) 338-2828
Fax Number: (0161) 338-8256
Ground Capacity: 6,108 **Seating Capacity**: 1,155
Web site: www.stalybridgeceltic.co.uk
E-mail: office@stalybridgeceltic.co.uk

GENERAL INFORMATION

Car Parking: At the ground (£1.00 charge)
Coach Parking: At the ground
Nearest Railway Station: Stalybridge (1 mile)
Nearest Bus Station: Stalybridge town centre
Club Shop: At the ground and also at "Stitch in Time", Market Street, Stalybridge
Opening Times: Matchdays only at the ground Monday to Friday 9.00am to 5.00pm at Market Street
Telephone Nº: (0161) 338-2828

GROUND INFORMATION

Away Supporters' Entrances & Sections:
Lockwood & Greenwood Stand on the few occasions when segregation is required. No usual segregation

ADMISSION INFO (2012/2013 PRICES)

Adult Standing: £10.00
Adult Seating: £10.00
Concessionary Standing: £6.00
Concessionary Seating: £6.00
Note: Under-12s are admitted for £1.00 when accompanied by a paying adult

DISABLED INFORMATION

Wheelchairs: 20 spaces available each for home and away fans at the side of the Stepan Stand. A further 9 spaces available in the new Lord Tom Pendry Stand
Helpers: Please phone the club for information
Prices: Please phone the club for information
Disabled Toilets: Available at the rear of the Stepan Stand and at the side of the Lord Tom Pendry Stand
Contact: (0161) 338-2828   (Bookings are necessary)

Travelling Supporters' Information:
Routes: From the Midlands and South: Take the M6, M56, M60 and M67, leaving at the end of the motorway. Go across the roundabout to the traffic lights and turn left. The ground is approximately 2 miles on the left before the Hare & Hounds pub; From the North: Exit the M62 at Junction 18 onto the M60 singposted for Ashton-under-Lyne. Follow the M60 to Junction 24 and join the M67, then as from the Midlands and South.

VAUXHALL MOTORS FC

Founded: 1963
Former Names: Vauxhall GM FC
Nickname: 'Motormen'
Ground: Rivacre Park, Rivacre Road, Hooton, Ellesmere Port, Cheshire   CH66 1NJ
Record Attendance: 1,500 (1987)
Pitch Size: 117 × 78 yards

Colours: White shirts with Blue shorts
Telephone Nº: (0151) 328-1114 (Ground)
Fax Nº: (0151) 328-1114
Ground Capacity: 3,306
Seating Capacity: 266
Web site: www.vmfc.com

GENERAL INFORMATION
Car Parking: At the ground
Coach Parking: At the ground
Nearest Railway Station: Overpool
Nearest Bus Station: Ellesmere Port
Club Shop: At the ground
Opening Times: Matchdays only
Telephone Nº: None

GROUND INFORMATION
Away Supporters' Entrances & Sections:
No usual segregation

ADMISSION INFO (2012/2013 PRICES)
Adult Standing: £9.00
Adult Seating: £9.00
Child Standing: £1.00
Child Seating: £1.00
Senior Citizen Standing/Seating: £6.00
Student Standing/Seating: £3.00

DISABLED INFORMATION
Wheelchairs: Accommodated as necessary
Helpers: Admitted
Prices: Normal prices for the disabled. Free for carers
Disabled Toilets: Available
Contact: –   (Bookings are not necessary)

Travelling Supporters' Information:
Routes: Exit the M53 at Junction 5 and take the A41 towards Chester. Turn left at the first set of traffic lights into Hooton Green. Turn left at the first T-junction then right at the next T-junction into Rivacre Road. The ground is situated 250 yards on the right.

WORCESTER CITY FC

Founded: 1902
Former Names: Berwick Rangers FC
Nickname: 'The City'
Ground: St. George's Lane, Worcester WR1 1QT
Record Attendance: 17,042 (1958/59)
Pitch Size: 110 × 75 yards

Colours: Blue and White shirts with Blue shorts
Telephone Nº: (01905) 23003
Fax Number: (01905) 26668
Ground Capacity: 4,500
Seating Capacity: 1,100
Web site: www.worcestercityfc.co.uk
E-mail: office@worcestercityfc.co.uk

GENERAL INFORMATION
Car Parking: Street parking
Coach Parking: Street parking
Nearest Railway Station: Foregate Street (1 mile)
Nearest Bus Station: Crowngate Bus Station
Club Shop: At the ground
Opening Times: Monday to Friday and Matchdays from 10.00am to 5.00pm
Telephone Nº: (01905) 23003

GROUND INFORMATION
Away Supporters' Entrances & Sections:
Turnstile at the Canal End when segregation is in force for Canal End accommodation

ADMISSION INFO (2012/2013 PRICES)
Adult Standing: £12.00
Adult Seating: £14.00
Under-16s Standing: £3.00
Under-16s Seating: £5.00
Senior Citizen Standing: £8.00
Senior Citizen Seating: £10.00

DISABLED INFORMATION
Wheelchairs: 3 covered spaces available
Helpers: Admitted
Prices: Normal prices apply for the disabled. Helpers are admitted free of charge
Disabled Toilets: None
Contact: (01905) 23003   (Bookings are necessary)

Travelling Supporters' Information:
Routes: Exit the M5 at Junction 6 and take the A449 Kidderminster Road. Follow to the end of the dual carriageway and take the second exit at the roundabout for Worcester City Centre. At the first set of traffic lights turn right into the town centre. The 3rd turning on the left is St. George's Lane North.

WORKINGTON AFC

Founded: 1884 (Reformed 1921)
Former Names: None
Nickname: 'Reds'
Ground: Borough Park, Workington   CA14 2DT
Record Attendance: 21,000 (vs Manchester United)
Pitch Size: 112 × 72 yards

Colours: Red shirts with White shorts
Telephone Nº: (01900) 602871
Fax Number: (01900) 67432
Ground Capacity: 3,100
Seating Capacity: 500
Web site: www.workingtonafc.com
E-mail: workington.reds@tiscali.co.uk

GENERAL INFORMATION

Car Parking: Car Park next to the ground
Coach Parking: At the ground
Nearest Railway Station: Workington (¼ mile)
Nearest Bus Station: Workington (½ mile)
Club Shop: At the ground
Opening Times: Matchdays only
Telephone Nº: (01946) 832710

GROUND INFORMATION

Away Supporters' Entrances & Sections:
No usual segregation

ADMISSION INFO (2012/2013 PRICES)

Adult Standing: £12.00
Adult Seating: £12.00
Senior Citizen/Junior/Student Standing: £7.00
Senior Citizen/Junior/Student Seating: £7.00
Note: Under-5s are admitted free of charge

DISABLED INFORMATION

Wheelchairs: Accommodated
Helpers: Admitted
Prices: Normal prices apply
Disabled Toilets: Available
Contact: (01900) 602871   (Bookings are not necessary)

Travelling Supporters' Information:
Routes: Exit the M6 at Junction 40 and take the A66 towards Keswick and Workington. Upon reaching Workington, continue until you reach the traffic lights at the bottom of the hill (with HSBC Bank facing) and turn left towards the town centre. Approach the traffic lights in the middle lane with the Washington Central Hotel on the right and turn right. Continue along this road, crossing a mini-roundabout, a pedestrian crossing and a further set of traffic lights. Upon reaching the railway station, pass through the junction and bear right passing the Derwent Park Rugby League Stadium then bear left and Borough Park is straight ahead.

THE FOOTBALL CONFERENCE BLUE SQUARE SOUTH

Address

Third Floor, Wellington House,
31-34 Waterloo Street, Birmingham   B2 5TJ

Phone (0121) 214-1950

Web site   www.footballconference.co.uk

Clubs for the 2012/2013 Season

AFC HORNCHURCH

Founded: 1923
Former Names: Hornchurch & Upminster FC and Hornchurch FC
Nickname: 'Urchins'
Ground: The Stadium, Bridge Avenue, Upminster, RM14 2LX
Record Attendance: 3,000 (vs Chelmsford 1966/67)

Colours: Red and White striped shirts, White shorts
Telephone Nº: (01708) 220080
Ground Capacity: 3,000
Seating Capacity: 499
Web site: www.urchins.org.uk

GENERAL INFORMATION
Car Parking: 100 spaces available at the ground
Coach Parking: At the ground
Nearest Railway Station: Upminster (10 minutes walk)
Nearest Tube Station: Upminster Bridge (5 minutes walk)
Club Shop: At the ground
Opening Times: Matchdays only
Telephone Nº: (01708) 220080

GROUND INFORMATION
Away Supporters' Entrances & Sections:
No usual segregation

ADMISSION INFO (2012/2013 PRICES)
Adult Standing: £11.00
Adult Seating: £11.00
Senior Citizen Standing: £7.00
Senior Citizen Seating: £7.00
Under-16s Standing: £3.00
Under-16s Seating: £3.00

DISABLED INFORMATION
Wheelchairs: Accommodated
Helpers: Admitted
Prices: £6.00 for the disabled
Disabled Toilets: Available
Contact: (01708) 220080 (Bookings are not necessary)

Travelling Supporters' Information:
Routes: Exit the M25 at Junction 29 and take the A127 towards London. After about 500 yards, take the sliproad signposted for Upminster/Cranham and continue on for about 1 mile. Turn right at the traffic lights by the church and Bridge Avenue is the 2nd turning on the left after about 400 yards.

BASINGSTOKE TOWN FC

Founded: 1896
Former Names: None
Nickname: 'Dragons'
Ground: The Camrose Ground, Western Way, Basingstoke, Hants.   RG22 6EZ
Record Attendance: 5,085 (25th November 1997)
Pitch Size: 110 × 70 yards

Colours: Yellow and Blue shirts with Blue shorts
Telephone Nº: (01256) 327575
Fax Number: (01256) 326346
Social Club Nº: (01256) 464353
Ground Capacity: 6,000
Seating Capacity: 650
Web site: www.basingstoketown.net
E-mail: richard.trodd@ntlworld.com

GENERAL INFORMATION

Car Parking: 600 spaces available at the ground (£1.00)
Coach Parking: Ample room available at ground
Nearest Railway Station: Basingstoke
Nearest Bus Station: Basingstoke Town Centre (2 miles)
Club Shop: The Camrose Shop
Opening Times: Matchdays only
Telephone Nº: (01256) 327575

GROUND INFORMATION

Away Supporters' Entrances & Sections:
No usual segregation

ADMISSION INFO (2012/2013 PRICES)

Adult Standing: £12.00
Adult Seating: £13.00
Concessionary Standing: £8.00
Concessionary Seating: £9.00
Under-16s Standing: £4.00
Under-16s Seating: £5.00
Under-11s Standing: £1.00
Under-11s Seating: £2.00

DISABLED INFORMATION

Wheelchairs: 6 spaces are available under cover
Helpers: Admitted
Prices: Normal prices for the disabled. Free for helpers
Disabled Toilets: Yes
Contact: (01256) 327575   (Bookings are not necessary)

Travelling Supporters' Information:
Routes: Exit the M3 at Junction 6 and take the 1st left at the Black Dam roundabout. At the next roundabout take the 2nd exit, then the 1st exit at the following roundabout and the 5th exit at the next roundabout. This takes you into Western Way and the ground is 50 yards on the right.

BATH CITY FC

Founded: 1889
Former Names: Bath AFC, Bath Railway FC and Bath Amateurs FC
Nickname: 'The Romans'
Ground: Twerton Park, Bath   BA2 1DB
Record Attendance: 18,020 (1960)
Pitch Size: 110 × 76 yards

Colours: Black and White striped shirts, Black shorts
Telephone Nº: (01225) 423087/313247
Fax Number: (01225) 481391
Ground Capacity: 8,840
Seating Capacity: 1,026
Web site: www.bathcityfc.com

GENERAL INFORMATION
Car Parking: 150 spaces available at the ground
Coach Parking: Available at the ground
Nearest Railway Station: Oldfield Park (1 mile)
Nearest Bus Station: Avon Street, Bath
Club Shop: Yes – contact Martin Brush, c/o Club
Opening Times: Matchdays and office hours
Telephone Nº: (01225) 423087

GROUND INFORMATION
Away Supporters' Entrances & Sections:
Turnstiles 17-19

ADMISSION INFO (2012/2013 PRICES)
Adult Standing: £12.00
Adult Seating: £13.00
Senior Citizen Standing: £8.00
Senior Citizen Seating: £9.00
Under-16s Standing: £6.00
Under-16s Seating: £7.00

DISABLED INFORMATION
Wheelchairs: 10 spaces available each for home and away fans in front of the Family Stand
Helpers: Admitted
Prices: £9.00 for the disabled. Free entrance for helpers
Disabled Toilets: Available behind the Family Stand
Contact: (01225) 423087   (Bookings are not necessary)

Travelling Supporters' Information:
Route: As a recommendation, avoid exiting the M4 at Junction 18 as the road from takes you through Bath City Centre. Instead, exit the M4 at Junction 19 onto the M32. Turn off the M32 at Junction 1 and follow the A4174 Bristol Ring Road south then join the A4 for Bath. On the A4, after passing through Saltford you will reach a roundabout shortly before entering Bath. Take the 2nd exit at this roundabout then follow the road before turning left into Newton Road at the bottom of the steep hill. The ground is then on the right hand side of the road.

BILLERICAY TOWN FC

Founded: 1880
Former Names: None
Nickname: 'Town' 'Blues'
Ground: New Lodge, Blunts Wall Road, Billericay, Essex   CM12 9SA
Record Attendance: 3,841 (28th September 1977)

Colours: Shirts are Royal Blue with White trim, shorts are White with Royal Blue trim
Telephone Nº: (01277) 652188
Fax Number: (01277) 652188
Ground Capacity: 3,500
Seating Capacity: 424
Web site: www.billericaytownfc.co.uk

GENERAL INFORMATION

Car Parking: 50 spaces available at the training ground behind the stadium
Coach Parking: Please contact the club for information
Nearest Railway Station: Billericay (½ mile)
Club Shop: At the ground
Opening Times: Matchdays only

GROUND INFORMATION

Away Supporters' Entrances & Sections:
No usual segregation

ADMISSION INFO (2012/2013 PRICES)

Adult Standing: £9.50
Adult Seating: £10.50
Senior Citizen Standing: £6.50
Senior Citizen Seating: £7.50
Under-16s Standing: £2.50
Under-16s Seating: £3.50

DISABLED INFORMATION

Wheelchairs: Accommodated
Helpers: Admitted
Prices: Same prices as standing admission
Disabled Toilets: Available in the Clubhouse
Contact: (01277) 652188   (Bookings are necessary)

Travelling Supporters' Information:
Route: Exit the M25 at Junction 28 and follow the A129 to Billericay. Turn right at the 1st set of traffic lights into Tye Common Road then 2nd right into Blunts Wall Road and the ground is on the right.
Alternative route: Exit the M25 at Junction 29 and take the A129 road from Basildon into Billericay and turn left at the 2nd set of traffic lights into Tye Common Road. Then as above.

BOREHAM WOOD FC

Founded: 1948
Former Names: Boreham Rovers FC and Royal Retournez FC
Nickname: 'The Wood'
Ground: Meadow Park, Broughinge Road, Boreham Wood, Hertfordshire WD6 5AL
Record Attendance: 4,030 (2002)
Pitch Size: 112 × 72 yards

Colours: White shirts with Black shorts
Telephone Nº: (0208) 953-5097
Fax Number: (0208) 207-7982
Ground Capacity: 4,239
Seating Capacity: 500
Web site: www.borehamwoodfootballclub.co.uk

GENERAL INFORMATION
Car Parking: At the ground
Coach Parking: At the ground
Nearest Railway Station: Elstree & Boreham Wood (1 mile)
Nearest Bus Station: Barnet
Club Shop: At the ground
Opening Times: 11.00am to 10.00pm Monday to Thursday; 11.00am to 6.00pm at weekends
Telephone Nº: (0208) 953-5097

GROUND INFORMATION
Away Supporters' Entrances & Sections:
No usual segregation

ADMISSION INFO (2012/2013 PRICES)
Adult Standing: £11.00
Adult Seating: £11.00
Child Standing: £6.00
Child Seating: £6.00

DISABLED INFORMATION
Wheelchairs: Accommodated
Helpers: Admitted
Prices: Concessionary prices are charged for the disabled and helpers
Disabled Toilets: None
Contact: (0208) 953-5097 (Bookings are necessary)

Travelling Supporters' Information:
Routes: Exit the M25 at Junction 23 and take the A1 South. After 2 miles, take the Boreham Wood exit onto the dual carriageway and go over the flyover following signs for Boreham Wood for 1 mile. Turn right at the Studio roundabout into Brook Road, then next right into Broughinge Road for the ground.

BROMLEY FC

Founded: 1892
Former Names: None
Nickname: 'Lillywhites'
Ground: The Stadium, Hayes Lane, Bromley, Kent, BR2 9EF
Record Attendance: 12,000 (24th September 1949)
Pitch Size: 112 × 72 yards

Colours: White shirts with Black shorts
Telephone Nº: (020) 8460-5291
Fax Number: (020) 8313-3992
Ground Capacity: 3,300
Seating Capacity: 1,300
Web site: www.bromleyfc.net
E-mail: info@bromleyfc.net

GENERAL INFORMATION
Car Parking: 300 spaces available at the ground
Coach Parking: At the ground
Nearest Railway Station: Bromley South (1 mile)
Nearest Bus Station: High Street, Bromley
Club Shop: At the ground
Opening Times: Matchdays only
Telephone Nº: (020) 8460-5291

GROUND INFORMATION
Away Supporters' Entrances & Sections:
No usual segregation

ADMISSION INFO (2012/2013 PRICES)
Adult Standing/Seating: £12.00
Concessionary Standing/Seating: £6.00
Under-16s/Student Standing/Seating: £5.00
Note: Under-5s are admitted free of charge

DISABLED INFORMATION
Wheelchairs: Accommodated
Helpers: Admitted
Prices: Please phone the club for information
Disabled Toilets: Yes
Contact: (0181) 460-5291 (Bookings are necessary)

Travelling Supporters' Information:
Routes: Exit the M25 at Junction 4 and follow the A21 for Bromley and London for approximately 4 miles before forking left onto the A232 signposted for Croydon/Sutton. At the second set of traffic lights turn right into Baston Road (B265) and follow for approximately 2 miles as it becomes Hayes Street and then Hayes Lane. The ground is on the right just after a mini-roundabout.

CHELMSFORD CITY FC

Founded: 1938
Former Names: Chelmsford FC
Nickname: 'City' or 'Clarets'
Ground: Melbourne Park, Salerno Way, Chelmsford, CM1 2EH
Record Attendance: 16,807 (at previous ground)
Pitch Size: 109 × 70 yards

Colours: Claret and White shirts and shorts
Telephone Nº: (01245) 290959
Ground Capacity: 3,000
Seating Capacity: 1,400
Web site: www.chelmsfordcityfc.com

GENERAL INFORMATION

Car Parking: Limited space at ground and street parking
Coach Parking: Two spaces available at the ground subject to advance notice
Nearest Railway Station: Chelmsford (2 miles)
Nearest Bus Station: Chelmsford (2 miles)
Club Shop: At the ground
Opening Times: Matchdays only at present
Telephone Nº: (01245) 290959

GROUND INFORMATION

Away Supporters' Entrances & Sections:
No usual segregation

ADMISSION INFO (2012/2013 PRICES)

Adult Standing: £11.50
Adult Seating: £12.50
Under-16s Standing: £3.50
Under-16s Seating: £4.50
Under-12s Standing: Free of charge
Under-12s Seating: £1.00
Concessionary Standing: £7.50
Concessionary Seating: £8.50

DISABLED INFORMATION

Wheelchairs: Spaces for 11 wheelchairs available
Helpers: Admitted free of charge
Prices: Disabled fans are charged standing admission prices
Disabled Toilets: Available
Contact: (01245) 290959 (Bookings are necessary)

Travelling Supporters' Information:
Route: The ground is situated next to the only set of high rise flats in Chelmsford which can therefore be used as a landmark. From the A12 from London: Exit the A12 at Junction 15 signposted for Chelmsford/Harlow/A414 and head towards Chelmsford along the dual-carriageway. At the third roundabout, immediately after passing the 'Superbowl' on the left, take the first exit into Westway, signposted for the Crematorium and Widford Industrial Estate. Continue along Westway which becomes Waterhouse Lane after the second set of traffic lights. At the next set of lights (at the gyratory system) take the first exit into Rainsford Road, signposted for Sawbridgeworth A1060. Continue along Rainsford Road then turn right into Chignal Road at the second set of traffic lights. Turn right again into Melbourne Avenue and Salerno Way is on the left at the end of the football pitches.

DORCHESTER TOWN FC

Founded: 1880
Former Names: None
Nickname: 'The Magpies'
Ground: The Avenue Stadium, Weymouth Avenue, Dorchester, Dorset DT1 2RY
Record Attendance: 4,159 (1st January 1999)
Pitch Size: 110 × 80 yards

Colours: Black and White striped shirts with Black shorts and socks
Telephone Nº: (01305) 262451
Fax Number: (01305) 267623
Ground Capacity: 5,009
Seating Capacity: 710
Web Site: www.dorchestertownfc.co.uk
E-mail: manager@dorchestertownfc.co.uk

GENERAL INFORMATION

Car Parking: 350 spaces available at the ground (£1.00 fee)
Coach Parking: At the ground
Nearest Railway Station: Dorchester South and West (both 1 mile)
Nearest Bus Station: Nearby
Club Shop: At the ground
Opening Times: During 1st team matchdays only
Telephone Nº: (01305) 262451

GROUND INFORMATION

Away Supporters' Entrances & Sections:
Main Stand side when segregated (not usual)

ADMISSION INFO (2012/2013 PRICES)

Adult Standing: £10.00
Adult Seating: £11.00
Senior Citizen Standing: £6.50
Senior Citizen Seating: £7.50
Under-19s Standing/Seating: £5.00
Under-10s Standing/Seating: £3.00

DISABLED INFORMATION

Wheelchairs: 10 spaces available each for home and away fans at the North West End of the terracing
Helpers: Admitted
Prices: Normal prices apply
Disabled Toilets: 2 available near the disabled area
Contact: (01305) 262451 (Bookings are not necessary)

Travelling Supporters' Information:
Routes: Take the Dorchester Bypass (A35) from all directions. The ground is on the South side of town, adjacent to a roundabout at the intersection with the A354 to Weymouth. Alternatively, take Weymouth signs from Dorchester Town Centre for 1½ miles.

DOVER ATHLETIC FC

Founded: 1983
Former Names: None
Nickname: 'The Whites'
Ground: Crabble Athletic Ground, Lewisham Road, River, Dover CT17 0JB
Record Attendance: 4,186 (2002)
Pitch Size: 111 × 73 yards

Colours: White shirts with Black shorts
Telephone Nº: (01304) 822373
Fax Number: (01304) 821383
Ground Capacity: 6,500
Seating Capacity: 1,000
Web site: www.dover-athletic.com
E-mail: enquiries@doverathletic.com

GENERAL INFORMATION
Car Parking: Street parking
Coach Parking: Street parking
Nearest Railway Station: Kearsney (1 mile)
Nearest Bus Station: Pencester Road, Dover (1½ miles)
Club Shop: At the ground
Opening Times: Saturdays 9.00am to 12.00pm
Telephone Nº: (01304) 822373

GROUND INFORMATION
Away Supporters' Entrances & Sections:
Segregation only used when required

ADMISSION INFO (2012/2013 PRICES)
Adult Standing: £12.00
Adult Seating: £13.50
Senior Citizen Standing: £9.00
Senior Citizen Seating: £10.00
Under-18s Standing: £6.00   (Under-11s £3.00)
Under-18s Seating: £7.50   (Under-11s £3.00)

DISABLED INFORMATION
Wheelchairs: Approximately 20 spaces are available in front of the Family Stand
Helpers: Please phone the club for information
Prices: Please phone the club for information
Disabled Toilets: None
Contact: –   (Bookings are not necessary)

Travelling Supporters' Information:
Routes: Take the A2 to the Whitfield roundabout and take the 4th exit. Travel down the hill to the mini-roundabout then turn left and follow the road for 1 mile to the traffic lights on the hill. Turn sharp right and pass under the railway bridge – the ground is on the left after 300 yards.

EASTBOURNE BOROUGH FC

Founded: 1963
Former Names: Langney Sports FC
Nickname: 'The Sports'
Ground: Langney Sports Club, Priory Lane,
Eastbourne   BN23 7QH
Record Attendance: 3,770 (5th November 2005)
Pitch Size: 115 × 72 yards

Colours: Red shirts with Black shorts
Telephone Nº: (01323) 766265
Fax Number: (01323) 741627
Ground Capacity: 4,400
Seating Capacity: 542
Web site: www.ebfc.co.uk

GENERAL INFORMATION

Car Parking: Around 400 spaces available at the ground
Coach Parking: At the ground
Nearest Railway Station: Pevensey & Westham (1½ miles but no public transport to the ground)
Nearest Bus Station: Eastbourne   (Service 6A to ground)
Club Shop: At the ground
Opening Times: Matchdays only
Telephone Nº: (01323) 766265

GROUND INFORMATION

Away Supporters' Entrances & Sections:
No usual segregation

ADMISSION INFO (2012/2013 PRICES)

Adult Standing: £12.00
Adult Seating: £12.00
Under-16s Standing: £1.00
Under-16s Seating: £1.00
Senior Citizen Standing: £8.00
Senior Citizen Seating: £8.00

DISABLED INFORMATION

Wheelchairs: 6 spaces available
Helpers: Admitted
Prices: Normal prices apply
Disabled Toilets: Available
Contact: (01323) 766265   (Bookings are necessary)

Travelling Supporters' Information:
Routes: From the North: Exit the A22 onto the Polegate bypass, signposted A27 Eastbourne, Hastings & Bexhill. *Take the 2nd exit at the next roundabout for Stone Cross and Westham (A22) then the first exit at the following roundabout signposted Stone Cross and Westham. Turn right after ½ mile into Friday Street (B2104). At the end of Friday Street, turn left at the double mini-roundabout into Hide Hollow (B2191), passing Eastbourne Crematorium on your right. Turn right at the roundabout into Priory Road, and Priory Lane is about 200 yards down the road on the left; Approaching on the A27 from Brighton: Turn left at the Polegate traffic lights then take 2nd exit at the large roundabout to join the bypass. Then as from *.

EASTLEIGH FC

Founded: 1946
Former Names: Swaythling Athletic FC and Swaythling FC
Nickname: 'The Spitfires'
Ground: Silverlake Stadium, Ten Acres, Stoneham Lane, Eastleigh SO50 9HT
Record Attendance: 3,104 (2006)
Pitch Size: 112 × 74 yards

Colours: White shirts with Royal Blue shorts
Telephone Nº: (023) 8061-3361
Fax Number: (023) 8061-2379
Ground Capacity: 3,000
Seating Capacity: 512
Web site: www.eastleigh-fc.co.uk
e-mail: commercial@eastleigh-fc.co.uk

GENERAL INFORMATION

Car Parking: Spaces for 450 cars available (hard standing)
Coach Parking: At the ground
Nearest Railway Station: Southampton Parkway (¾ mile)
Nearest Bus Station: Eastleigh (2 miles)
Club Shop: At the ground
Opening Times: Matchdays and during functions only

GROUND INFORMATION

Away Supporters' Entrances & Sections:
No usual segregation

ADMISSION INFO (2012/2013 PRICES)

Adult Standing/Seating: £12.00
Concessionary Standing/Seating: £7.50
Under-16s Standing/Seating: £4.00
Under-12s Standing/Seating: Free of charge

DISABLED INFORMATION

Wheelchairs: Accommodated
Helpers: Admitted
Prices: Normal prices apply
Disabled Toilets: Available
Contact: (023) 8061-3361 (Bookings are not necessary)

Travelling Supporters' Information:
Routes: Exit the M27 at Junction 5 (signposted for Southampton Airport) and take the A335 (Stoneham Way) towards Southampton. After ½ mile, turn right at the traffic lights into Bassett Green Road. Turn right at the next set of traffic lights into Stoneham Lane and the ground is on the right after ¾ mile.

FARNBOROUGH FC

Founded: 1967   (Re-formed in 2007)
Former Names: Farnborough Town FC
Nickname: 'The Boro'
Ground: The Rushmoor Stadium, Cherrywood Road, Farnborough   GU14 8UD
Record Attendance: 4,267 (15th May 2011)
Pitch Size: 115 × 77 yards

Colours: Yellow and Blue shirts and shorts
Telephone Nº: 0844 807-9900
Fax Number: (01252) 372640
Ground Capacity: 5,600 at present
Seating Capacity: 3,135
Web site: www.farnboroughfc.co.uk
E-mail contact: admin@farnboroughfc.co.uk

GENERAL INFORMATION

Car Parking: 260 spaces available at the ground with a further 200 spaces at the nearby Sixth Form college
Coach Parking: At the ground
Nearest Railway Stations: Farnborough (Main), Farnborough North, Frimley and Blackwater
Nearest Bus Station: Buses from Farnborough Main stop just outside the ground – please check the web site for details.
Club Shop: At the ground + web sales in the near future
Opening Times: Matchdays only
Telephone Nº: 0844 807-8800

GROUND INFORMATION

Away Supporters' Entrances & Sections:
Moor Road entrances and accommodation

ADMISSION INFO (2012/2013 PRICES)

Adult Standing: £12.00
Adult Seating: £12.00
Concessionary Standing: £8.00
Concessionary Seating: £8.00
Under-16s Seating/Standing: £3.00
Under-6s Seating/Standing: Free of charge
Note: In keeping with F.A. Regulations, the Club reserves the right to charge higher prices for F.A. Trophy and F.A. Cup games.
Programme Price: £2.50

DISABLED INFORMATION

Wheelchairs: Spaces available in a disabled section in the PRE Stand
Helpers: Admitted free of charge
Prices: Concessionary prices charged for disabled fans
Disabled Toilets: Available in the PRE Stand
Contact: 0844 807-9900   (Bookings are not necessary)

Travelling Supporters' Information:
Routes: Exit the M3 at Junction 4 and take the A331 signposted for Farnham. After a few hundred yards exit at the second slip road – signposted A325 Farnborough – turn right at the roundabout and cross over the dual carriageway and a small roundabout. Pass the Farnborough Gate shopping centre on your left and at the next roundabout turn left onto the A325. Go over a pelican crossing and at the next set of lights take the right filter lane into Prospect Avenue. At the end of this road turn right at the roundabout into Cherrywood Road. The ground is on the right after ½ mile.

HAVANT & WATERLOOVILLE FC

Founded: 1998
Former Names: Formed by the amalgamation of Waterlooville FC and Havant Town FC
Nickname: 'The Hawks'
Ground: Westleigh Park, Martin Road, Havant, PO9 5TH
Record Attendance: 5,757 (2006/07)
Pitch Size: 112 × 76 yards

Colours: White shirts and shorts
Telephone Nº: (023) 9278-7822 (Ground)
Fax Number: (023) 9226-2367
Ground Capacity: 5,250
Seating Capacity: 562
Web site: www.havantandwaterlooville.net

GENERAL INFORMATION
Car Parking: Space for 750 cars at the ground
Coach Parking: At the ground
Nearest Railway Station: Havant (1 mile)
Nearest Bus Station: Town Centre (1½ miles)
Club Shop: At the ground
Opening Times: Daily
Telephone Nº: (023) 9278-7822

GROUND INFORMATION
Away Supporters' Entrances & Sections:
Martin Road End

ADMISSION INFO (2012/2013 PRICES)
Adult Standing: £12.00
Adult Seating: £12.00
Senior Citizen Standing/Seating: £7.00
Concessionary Standing/Seating: £7.00
Note: When accompanied by a paying adult, children under the age of 11 are admitted free of charge

DISABLED INFORMATION
Wheelchairs: 12 spaces available in the Main Stand
Helpers: Admitted
Prices: Normal prices for disabled fans. Free for helpers
Disabled Toilets: Two available
Contact: (023) 9226-7276   (Bookings are necessary)

Travelling Supporters' Information:
Routes: From London or the North take the A27 from Chichester and exit at the B2149 turn-off for Havant. Take the 2nd exit off the dual carriageway into Bartons Road and then the 1st right into Martin Road for the ground; From the West: Take the M27 then the A27 to the Petersfield exit. Then as above.

HAYES & YEADING UNITED FC

Hayes & Yeading United FC are groundsharing with Woking FC for the early part of the 2012/2013 season but hope to be able to move into their new ground at Beaconsfield Road, Hayes, later in the year. Please contact the club for further details.

Founded: 2007
Former Names: Formed by the amalgamation of Hayes FC and Yeading FC in 2007
Nickname: 'United'
Ground: Kingfield Stadium, Kingfield, Woking, Surrey   GU22 9AA
Record Attendance: 6,000 (1997)
Pitch Size: 109 × 76 yards

Colours: Red Shirts with Black shorts
Telephone Nº: (020) 8756-1200
Fax Number: (020) 8756-1200
Ground Capacity: 6,161
Seating Capacity: 2,511
Web site: www.hyufc.com

GENERAL INFORMATION
Car Parking: Limited parking at the ground
Coach Parking: At or opposite the ground
Nearest Railway Station: Woking (1 mile)
Nearest Bus Station: Woking
Club Shop: None

GROUND INFORMATION
Away Supporters' Entrances & Sections:
Kingfield Road entrance for the Tennis Club terrace

ADMISSION INFO (2012/2013 PRICES)
Adult Standing: £12.00
Adult Seating: £12.00
Under-16s/Student Standing: £2.00
Under-16s/Student Seating: £2.00
Senior Citizen Standing: £8.00
Senior Citizen Seating: £8.00

DISABLED INFORMATION
Wheelchairs: 8 spaces in the Leslie Gosden Stand and 8 spaces in front of the Family Stand
Helpers: Admitted
Prices: One wheelchair and helper for £8.00
Disabled Toilets: Yes – in the Leslie Gosden Stand and Family Stand area
Contact: (020) 8756-1200   (Bookings are necessary)

Travelling Supporters' Information:
Routes: Exit the M25 at Junction 10 and follow the A3 towards Guildford. Leave at the next junction onto the B2215 through Ripley and join the A247 to Woking. Alternatively, exit the M25 at Junction 11 and follow the A320 to Woking Town Centre. The ground is on the outskirts of Woking – follow signs on the A320 and A247.

MAIDENHEAD UNITED FC

Founded: 1870
Former Names: None
Nickname: 'Magpies'
Ground: York Road, Maidenhead, Berks. SL6 1SF
Record Attendance: 7,920 (1936)
Pitch Size: 110 × 75 yards

Colours: Black and White striped shirts, Black shorts
Telephone Nº: (01628) 636314 (Club)
Contact Number: (01628) 636078
Ground Capacity: 4,500
Seating Capacity: 400
Web: www.pitchero.com/clubs/maidenheadunited/

GENERAL INFORMATION
Car Parking: Street parking
Coach Parking: Street parking
Nearest Railway Station: Maidenhead (¼ mile)
Nearest Bus Station: Maidenhead
Club Shop: At the ground
Opening Times: Matchdays only
Telephone Nº: (01628) 624739

GROUND INFORMATION
Away Supporters' Entrances & Sections:
No usual segregation

ADMISSION INFO (2012/2013 PRICES)
Adult Standing: £10.00
Adult Seating: £10.00
Concessionary Standing and Seating: £6.00
Under-18s Standing and Seating: £2.00
Note: Junior Magpies (Under-16s) are admitted free

DISABLED INFORMATION
Wheelchairs: Accommodated
Helpers: Admitted
Prices: Normal prices for the disabled. Free for helpers
Disabled Toilets: Available
Contact: (01628) 636078 (Bookings are not necessary)

Travelling Supporters' Information:
Routes: Exit M4 at Junction 7 and take the A4 to Maidenhead. Cross the River Thames bridge and turn left at the 2nd roundabout passing through the traffic lights. York Road is first right and the ground is approximately 300 yards along on the left.

SALISBURY CITY FC

Founded: 1947
Former Names: Salisbury FC
Nickname: 'The Whites'
Ground: The Raymond McEnhill Stadium, Partridge Way, Old Sarum, Salisbury, Wiltshire SP4 6PU
Record Attendance: 3,100 (8th December 2006)
Pitch Size: 115 × 76 yards

Colours: White shirts and shorts
Telephone Nº: (01722) 776655
Fax Number: (01722) 323100
Ground Capacity: 5,000
Seating Capacity: 500
Web site: www.salisburycity-fc.co.uk
E-mail: info@salisburycity-fc.co.uk

GENERAL INFORMATION
Car Parking: At the ground
Coach Parking: At the ground
Nearest Railway Station: Salisbury (2½ miles)
Nearest Bus Station: Salisbury
Club Shop: At the ground + an online shop
Opening Times: Office Hours and Matchdays
Telephone Nº: (01722) 776655
Postal Sales: Yes

GROUND INFORMATION
Away Supporters' Entrances & Sections:
No usual segregation

ADMISSION INFO (2012/2013 PRICES)
Adult Standing: £13.00
Adult Seating: £15.00
Senior Citizen/Concessionary Standing: £10.00
Senior Citizen/Concessionary Seating: £12.00
Under-16s Standing: £3.00
Under-16s Seating: £5.00

DISABLED INFORMATION
Wheelchairs: Accommodated in a special area in the Main Stand. A stairlift is available.
Helpers: Admitted free of charge
Prices: Normal prices apply for the disabled
Disabled Toilets: Available
Contact: (01722) 776655   (Bookings are necessary)

Travelling Supporters' Information:
Routes: The Stadium well signposted and is situated off the main A345 Salisbury to Amesbury road on the northern edge of the City, 2 miles from the City Centre.

STAINES TOWN FC

Photograph courtesy of Laurence Wakefield

Founded: 1892
Former Names: Staines FC, Staines Vale FC, Staines Albany FC, Staines Projectile FC & Staines Lagonda FC
Nickname: 'The Swans'
Ground: Wheatsheaf Park, Wheatsheaf Lane, Staines TW18 2PD
Record Attendance: 2,860 (2007)
Pitch Size: 110 × 76 yards

Ground Capacity: 3,061
Seating Capacity: 500
Colours: Old Gold and Blue shirts with Blue shorts
Telephone Nº: 0782 506-7232
Correspondence Address: Steve Parsons, 3 Birch Green, Staines TW18 4HA
Web site: www.stainesmassive.co.uk

GENERAL INFORMATION
Car Parking: Large car park shared with The Thames Club
Coach Parking: At the ground
Nearest Railway Station: Staines (1 mile)
Nearest Bus Station: Staines Central (1 mile)
Club Shop: At the ground
Opening Times: Matchdays only
Telephone Nº: (01784) 463100

GROUND INFORMATION
Away Supporters' Entrances & Sections:
No usual segregation

ADMISSION INFO (2012/2013 PRICES)
Adult Standing: £12.00
Adult Seating: £12.00
Senior Citizen Standing/Seating: £6.00
Junior Standing/Seating: £5.00

DISABLED INFORMATION
Wheelchairs: Accommodated
Helpers: Admitted
Prices: Normal prices apply for the disabled
Disabled Toilets: Available
Contact: (01784) 225943

Travelling Supporters' Information:
Routes: Exit the M25 at Junction 13 and take the A30 towards London. At the 'Crooked Billet' roundabout follow signs for Staines Town Centre. Pass under the bridge and bear left, passing the Elmsleigh Centre Car Parks and bear left at the next junction (opposite the Thames Lodge Hotel) into Laleham Road. Pass under the iron railway bridge by the river and continue along for ¾ mile. Turn right by the bollards into Wheatsheaf Lane and the ground is situated on the left by the Thames Club.

SUTTON UNITED FC

Founded: 1898
Former Names: Formed by the amalgamation of Sutton Guild Rovers FC and Sutton Association FC
Nickname: 'U's'
Ground: Borough Sports Ground, Gander Green Lane, Sutton, Surrey   SM1   2EY
Record Attendance: 14,000 (1970)

Colours: Chocolate and Amber shirts with Chocolate-coloured shorts
Telephone Nº: (020) 8644-4440
Fax Number: (020) 8644-5120
Ground Capacity: 7,032
Seating Capacity: 765
Web site: www.suttonunited.net

GENERAL INFORMATION
Car Parking: 150 spaces behind the Main Stand
Coach Parking: Space for 1 coach in the car park
Nearest Railway Station: West Sutton (adjacent)
Club Shop: At the ground
Opening Times: Matchdays only
Telephone Nº: (020) 8644-4440

GROUND INFORMATION
Away Supporters' Entrances & Sections:
Collingwood Road entrances and accommodation

ADMISSION INFO (2012/2013 PRICES)
Adult Standing: £12.00
Adult Seating: £13.00
Child Standing: £2.00
Child Seating: £3.00
Senior Citizen Standing: £6.00
Senior Citizen Seating: £7.00

DISABLED INFORMATION
Wheelchairs: 8 spaces are available under cover accommodated on the track perimeter
Helpers: Admitted
Prices: Normal prices apply
Disabled Toilets: Available alongside the Standing Terrace
Contact: (020) 8644-4440 (Bookings are necessary)

Travelling Supporters' Information:
Routes: Exit the M25 at Junction 8 (Reigate Hill) and travel North on the A217 for approximately 8 miles. Cross the A232 then turn right at the traffic lights (past Goose & Granit Public House) into Gander Green Lane. The ground is 300 yards on the left; From London: Gander Green Lane crosses the Sutton bypass 1 mile south of Rose Hill Roundabout. Avoid Sutton Town Centre, especially on Saturdays.

TONBRIDGE ANGELS FC

Founded: 1948
Former Names: Tonbridge FC
Nickname: 'The Angels'
Ground: Longmead Stadium, Darenth Avenue, Tonbridge TN10 3JF
Record Attendance: 2,411 (2011)

Colours: Blue and White shirts with Blue shorts
Telephone Nº: (01732) 352417
Ground Capacity: 3,014
Seating Capacity: 774
Web site: www.tonbridgeangels.co.uk
E-mail: chcole1063@aol.com

GENERAL INFORMATION
Car Parking: At the ground
Coach Parking: At the ground
Nearest Railway Station: Tonbridge (2 miles)
Club Shop: At the ground
Opening Times: Matchdays only
Telephone Nº: (01732) 352417

GROUND INFORMATION
Away Supporters' Entrances & Sections:
No usual segregation

ADMISSION INFO (2012/2013 PRICES)
Adult Standing: £12.00
Adult Seating: £13.00
Student/Senior Citizen Standing: £6.00
Student/Senior Citizen Seating: £7.00
Under-12s Standing: £3.00
Under-12s Seating: £4.00
Note: Family Tickets are also available

DISABLED INFORMATION
Wheelchairs: Accommodated
Helpers: Admitted
Prices: Normal prices apply
Disabled Toilets: One available
Contact: (01732) 352417

Travelling Supporters' Information:
Routes: Take the A26 or A21 to Tonbridge Town Centre, pass through the High Street and head north up Shipbourne Road which is the A227 Gravesend road. Turn left at the 2nd mini-roundabout by the 'Pinnacles' Pub into Darenth Avenue. The ground is situated at the bottom end of Darenth Avenue.

TRURO CITY FC

Founded: 1889
Former Names: None
Nickname: 'White Tigers'
Ground: Treyew Road, Truro   TR1 2TH
Record Attendance: 2,637 (31st March 2007)
Colours: All White shirts and shorts

Telephone Nº: (01872) 225400
Fax Number: (01872) 225402
Ground Capacity: 3,000
Seating Capacity: 1,600
Web Site: www.trurocityfc.co.uk
E-mail: mark@tigermedical.co.uk

GENERAL INFORMATION
Car Parking: At the ground
Coach Parking: At the ground
Nearest Railway Station: Truro (½ mile)
Club Shop: None

GROUND INFORMATION
Away Supporters' Entrances & Sections:
No usual segregation

ADMISSION INFO (2012/2013 PRICES)
Adult Standing: £12.00
Adult Seating: £12.00
Concessionary Standing: £6.00
Concessionary Seating: £6.00
Under-12s Standing: £3.00
Under-12s Seating: £3.00

DISABLED INFORMATION
Wheelchairs: Accommodated
Helpers: Admitted
Prices: Normal prices apply for the disabled and helpers
Disabled Toilets: Available
Contact: (01872) 225400   (Bookings are not necessary)

Travelling Supporters' Information:
Routes: From the North or East: Take the A30 to the A390 (from the North) or travel straight on the A390 (from the East) to Truro. Continue on the A390 and pass through Truro. The ground is located just to the South West of Truro on the left hand side of the A390 just before the County Hall; From the West: Take the A390 to Truro. The ground is on the right hand side of the road shortly after crossing the railway line and passing the County Hall; From the South: Take the A39 to Truro. At the junction with the A390 turn left onto Green Lane and the ground is on the left hand side of the road after approximately ½ mile.

WELLING UNITED FC

Founded: 1963
Former Names: None
Nickname: 'The Wings'
Ground: Park View Road Ground, Welling, Kent, DA16 1SY
Record Attendance: 4,020 (1989/90)
Pitch Size: 112 × 72 yards

Colours: Shirts are Red with White facings, Red shorts
Telephone N°: (0208) 301-1196
Daytime Phone N°: (0208) 301-1196
Fax Number: (0208) 301-5676
Ground Capacity: 4,000
Seating Capacity: 500
Web site: www.wellingunited.com

GENERAL INFORMATION

Car Parking: Street parking only
Coach Parking: Outside of the ground
Nearest Railway Station: Welling (¾ mile)
Nearest Bus Station: Bexleyheath
Club Shop: At the ground
Opening Times: Matchdays only
Telephone N°: (0208) 301-1196

GROUND INFORMATION

Away Supporters' Entrances & Sections:
Accommodation in the Danson Park End

ADMISSION INFO (2012/2013 PRICES)

Adult Standing: £12.00
Adult Seating: £13.00
Senior Citizen/Child Standing: £7.00
Senior Citizen/Child Seating: £8.00
Under-12s Standing: £3.00
Under-12s Seating: £4.00

DISABLED INFORMATION

Wheelchairs: Accommodated at the side of the Main Stand
Helpers: Admitted
Prices: £6.00 for the disabled. Helpers pay normal prices
Disabled Toilets: Yes
Contact: (0208) 301-1196 (Bookings are not necessary)

Travelling Supporters' Information:
Routes: Take the A2 (Rochester Way) from London, then the A221 Northwards (Danson Road) to Bexleyheath. At the end turn left towards Welling along Park View Road and the ground is on the left.

WESTON-SUPER-MARE FC

Founded: 1899
Former Names: Christ Church Old Boys FC
Nickname: 'Seagulls'
Ground: Woodspring Stadium, Winterstoke Road,
Weston-super-Mare   BS24 9AA
Record Attendance: 2,623   (vs Woking in F.A. Cup)
Pitch Size: 110 × 70 yards

Colours: White shirts with Black shorts
Telephone Nº: (01934) 621618
Fax Number: (01934) 622704
Ground Capacity: 3,071
Seating Capacity: 320
Web site: www.weston-s-mareafc.co.uk

GENERAL INFORMATION
Car Parking: 140 spaces available at the ground
Coach Parking: At the ground
Nearest Railway Station: Weston-super-Mare (1½ miles)
Nearest Bus Station: Weston-super-Mare (1½ miles)
Club Shop: At the ground
Opening Times: Matchdays only
Telephone Nº: (01934) 621618

GROUND INFORMATION
Away Supporters' Entrances & Sections:
No usual segregation

ADMISSION INFO (2012/2013 PRICES)
Adult Standing/Seating: £10.00
Senior Citizen Standing/Seating: £6.00
Under-16s Standing/Seating: £6.00
Note: Under-10s are admitted for £1.00 when accompanied
by a paying adult or senior citizen

DISABLED INFORMATION
Wheelchairs: Accommodated in a special disabled section
Helpers: Admitted
Prices: Normal prices apply
Disabled Toilets: Two available
Contact: (01934) 621618   (Bookings are not necessary)

Travelling Supporters' Information:
Routes: Exit the M5 at Junction 21 and follow the dual carriageway (A370) to the 4th roundabout (Asda Winterstoke). Turn left,
go over the mini-roundabout and continue for 800 yards. The ground is on the right.

Blue Square Premier / Football Conference National — 2011/2012 Season

Home \ Away	AFC Telford United	Alfreton Town	Barrow	Bath City	Braintree Town	Cambridge United	Darlington	Ebbsfleet United	Fleetwood Town	Forest Green Rovers	Gateshead	Grimsby Town	Hayes & Yeading United	Kettering Town	Kidderminster Harriers	Lincoln City	Luton Town	Mansfield Town	Newport County	Southport	Stockport County	Tamworth	Wrexham	York City
AFC Telford United	■	1-0	1-0	2-1	1-0	1-2	3-3	0-2	1-4	2-0	1-2	0-0	1-1	3-1	2-1	1-2	0-2	0-0	2-1	0-1	1-1	1-0	0-2	0-0
Alfreton Town	0-0	■	2-1	2-1	0-1	2-1	3-1	2-2	1-4	1-6	1-1	2-5	3-2	1-1	0-2	1-3	0-0	3-6	3-2	0-0	6-1	5-2	1-4	0-2
Barrow	2-1	1-0	■	0-1	0-4	1-3	3-0	1-1	4-0	1-1	1-2	2-2	3-1	3-0	3-1	1-0	1-0	2-3	3-1	3-2	1-0	1-1	3-1	0-0
Bath City	3-1	0-3	0-1	■	1-1	3-4	2-0	2-3	1-4	0-2	4-2	2-2	0-1	0-1	1-2	2-1	1-1	1-1	3-2	1-2	0-2	0-2	0-2	0-1
Braintree Town	2-1	1-2	1-0	3-3	■	3-2	3-1	2-3	1-2	1-5	3-1	5-0	0-3	2-1	1-4	1-0	3-1	1-1	1-0	0-0	2-2	3-1	0-0	0-1
Cambridge United	1-0	3-0	1-0	1-1	2-0	■	2-0	2-0	2-0	1-1	0-1	0-1	2-1	2-0	1-2	2-0	1-1	1-2	1-1	3-0	2-2	0-1	1-1	0-1
Darlington	1-0	1-1	0-1	2-2	1-0	2-0	■	0-2	0-1	0-0	0-0	1-1	3-1	1-0	3-1	1-1	0-2	2-0	0-3	0-1	2-0	2-4	2-2	
Ebbsfleet United	3-2	1-2	1-2	3-0	1-1	0-0	1-3	■	1-3	1-1	0-1	3-1	3-1	1-0	3-3	2-3	2-2	0-3	1-1	1-2	2-1	3-0	0-5	1-2
Fleetwood Town	2-2	4-0	4-1	4-1	3-1	1-0	0-0	6-2	■	0-0	3-1	2-1	1-0	3-0	5-2	2-2	0-2	2-0	1-4	2-2	2-1	2-2	1-1	0-0
Forest Green Rovers	2-1	4-1	3-0	3-0	0-2	2-1	2-0	3-1	1-2	■	2-1	0-1	1-3	0-1	1-1	0-2	3-0	1-1	1-1	2-3	1-1	3-1	1-0	1-1
Gateshead	3-0	2-0	2-0	1-0	2-2	1-1	1-1	2-3	1-1	1-0	■	1-0	2-0	1-1	2-1	3-3	0-0	3-0	2-3	2-3	2-0	1-1	1-4	3-2
Grimsby Town	2-0	5-2	5-2	6-0	1-1	2-1	1-2	4-3	0-2	2-1	2-0	■	3-0	1-2	3-1	1-0	0-0	2-2	0-1	7-0	0-0	1-3		2-3
Hayes & Yeading United	0-0	3-1	1-1	1-1	1-2	0-0	3-2	1-2	1-3	2-0	2-3	1-2	■	1-0	1-3	1-2	2-2	1-3	0-4	0-2	1-2	1-0	0-2	2-4
Kettering Town	2-1	0-2	1-1	1-1	2-1	0-0	0-0	2-2	1-3	2-1	1-2	3-5		■	0-1	1-0	0-5	0-3	3-2	2-3	1-3	0-2	0-1	1-5
Kidderminster Harriers	2-2	3-1	1-2	4-1	5-4	0-3	3-1	2-2	0-2	1-0	2-3	1-1	3-1	6-1	■	1-1	1-2	0-3	3-2	2-0	1-1	2-0	0-1	1-1
Lincoln City	1-1	0-1	2-1	2-0	3-3	0-1	5-0	3-0	1-3	1-1	1-0	1-2	0-1	0-2	0-1	■	1-1	1-1	2-0	2-0	1-1	4-0	1-2	0-2
Luton Town	1-1	1-0	5-1	2-0	3-1	0-1	2-0	3-0	1-2	1-1	5-1	4-2	5-0	1-0		1-0	■	0-0	2-0	5-1	1-0	3-0	1-1	1-2
Mansfield Town	1-1	3-2	7-0	1-1	4-1	1-2	5-2	1-0	1-1	1-1	1-1	2-1	3-2	3-0	0-3	2-1	1-1	■	5-0	1-3	2-1	2-1	2-0	1-1
Newport County	0-0		0-2	1-0	3-4	1-2	0-0	0-1	0-1	0-0	1-0	0-0	4-0	3-1	1-3	0-1	0-1	1-0	■	0-3	1-1	1-2	0-1	2-1
Southport	3-2	2-1	2-1	2-1	0-4	1-0	2-0	3-3	0-6	1-3	1-3	1-2	0-0	1-2	2-2	3-3	3-1	1-1	5-0	■	1-1	0-0	1-1	
Stockport County	2-2	0-0	3-2	4-0	1-1	0-1	3-4	1-1	2-4	0-1	3-3	1-0	2-1	4-0	1-1	0-1	2-2	0-1	2-2	0-1	■	2-0	1-0	1-2
Tamworth	2-2	2-2	2-3	0-1	1-0	2-2	1-0	0-3	0-1	1-1	1-1	2-1	2-2	0-0	4-0	1-3	0-1	2-1	2-2	1-1		■	1-2	2-1
Wrexham	4-0	0-1	2-0	2-0	5-1	1-1	2-1	1-0	2-0	1-2	2-1	2-2	4-1	4-1	2-0	2-0	1-3	0-0	2-0	4-0	3-0		■	0-3
York City	0-1	0-1	3-1	1-0	6-2	2-2	2-2	3-2	0-1	1-0	1-2	2-1	2-0	7-0	2-3	3-0	2-2	1-1	1-2	2-1	1-1	1-2	2-1	■

Blue Square Premier (Football Conference)

Season 2011/2012

Team	P	W	D	L	F	A	Pts
Fleetwood Town	46	31	10	5	102	48	103
Wrexham	46	30	8	8	85	33	98
Mansfield Town	46	25	14	7	87	48	89
York City	46	23	14	9	81	45	83
Luton Town	46	22	15	9	78	42	81
Kidderminster Harriers	46	22	10	14	82	63	76
Southport	46	21	13	12	72	69	76
Gateshead	46	21	11	14	69	62	74
Cambridge United	46	19	14	13	57	41	71
Forest Green Rovers	46	19	13	14	66	45	70
Grimsby Town	46	19	13	14	79	60	70
Braintree Town	46	17	11	18	76	80	62
Barrow	46	17	9	20	62	76	60
Ebbsfleet United	46	14	12	20	69	84	54
Alfreton Town	46	15	9	22	62	86	54
Stockport County	46	12	15	19	58	74	51
Lincoln City	46	13	10	23	56	66	49
Tamworth	46	11	15	20	47	70	48
Newport County	46	11	14	21	53	65	47
AFC Telford United	46	10	16	20	45	65	46
Hayes & Yeading United	46	11	8	27	58	90	41
Darlington	46	11	13	22	47	73	36
Bath City	46	7	10	29	43	89	31
Kettering Town	46	8	9	29	40	100	30

Darlington had 10 points deducted for entering administration. At the end of the season they were relegated four divisions for exiting administration without a CVA.

Kettering Town had 3 points deducted for failing to pay football creditors. At the end of the season they resigned from the Football Conference, dropping down two divisions.

Promotion Play-offs

York City 1   Mansfield Town 1
Luton Town 2   Wrexham 0

Mansfield Town 0   York City .... 1 (aet.)
York City won 2-1 on aggregate
Wrexham 2   Luton Town 1
Luton Town won 3-2 on aggregate

Luton Town 1   York City 2

Promoted: Fleetwood Town and York City
Relegated: Hayes & Yeading United, Darlington, Bath City and Kettering Town

Blue Square North / Football Conference North 2011/2012 Season	Altrincham	Bishop's Stortford	Blyth Spartans	Boston United	Colwyn Bay	Corby Town	Droylsden	Eastwood Town	FC Halifax Town	Gainsborough Trinity	Gloucester City	Guiseley	Harrogate Town	Hinckley United	Histon	Hyde	Nuneaton Town	Solihull Moors	Stalybridge Celtic	Vauxhall Motors	Worcester City	Workington
Altrincham		0-2	2-1	6-1	3-4	1-1	5-1	2-0	1-1	2-3	1-2	2-2	5-2	2-2	3-0	1-3	2-0	1-1	2-1	3-2	4-1	1-1
Bishop's Stortford	1-0		3-3	0-1	0-2	0-2	5-0	4-0	1-3	1-1	3-2	4-1	3-4	5-0	0-2	0-1	0-3	1-0	0-3	2-0	1-1	1-1
Blyth Spartans	1-1	3-1		1-0	2-2	1-2	1-3	1-0	2-3	2-3	0-1	1-2	3-3	3-3	2-1	0-1	2-3	2-1	1-1	1-2	1-2	0-3
Boston United	1-1	0-2	1-1		2-2	1-1	2-1	4-2	0-0	1-2	2-0	3-3	0-2	2-0	1-1	0-2	0-0	0-1	3-2	1-2	2-3	2-1
Colwyn Bay	1-6	4-1	0-2	3-2		0-2	6-3	2-0	0-1	2-1	4-2	1-2	2-2	0-5	2-1	0-1	1-6	0-0	2-0	0-0	0-2	1-0
Corby Town	1-3	6-1	4-0	1-2	1-0		5-2	5-0	2-4	1-3	0-1	0-1	0-5	0-2	0-2	0-4	0-2	0-3	1-2	1-0	2-3	3-3
Droylsden	3-1	2-2	3-3	2-1	2-1	2-1		3-3	2-1	1-2	1-2	2-0	1-1	2-3	2-3	2-3	2-1	1-0	3-3	5-2	4-1	1-1
Eastwood Town	1-6	3-4	0-0	2-2	0-1	1-4	2-2		2-2	1-6	2-1	2-2	0-1	0-3	1-2	2-2	0-5	1-1	0-1	2-4	0-1	0-3
FC Halifax Town	2-4	0-1	3-0	3-2	1-1	1-3	2-1	2-1		2-2	0-0	1-2	3-1	6-1	4-0	3-2	0-3	0-0	2-2	1-5	2-1	3-1
Gainsborough Trinity	2-0	4-2	2-0	1-3	2-0	1-0	1-2	2-0	0-1		1-4	1-0	0-1	2-1	3-2	2-0	3-1	3-1	1-1	1-1	2-2	2-0
Gloucester City	1-1	0-2	4-0	1-3	0-1	0-0	1-3	2-0	1-3	0-2			2-1	1-0	2-2	0-1	1-2	1-0	1-2	2-1	3-1	2-0
Guiseley	3-2	0-1	5-0	2-1	2-0	3-0	4-3	1-2	3-4	2-0	3-2		2-1	3-0	2-2	2-0	1-1	3-1	1-1	4-1	4-1	2-1
Harrogate Town	3-2	1-1	0-0	0-2	4-0	6-2	0-0	2-1	0-0	2-1	2-0	0-4		2-1	0-0	0-3	0-2	1-1	1-1	1-2	0-2	0-0
Hinckley United	1-4	1-3	1-3	1-2	3-1	0-3	1-1	4-0	3-2	2-3	0-1	1-2			0-3	1-0	1-1	1-2	5-5	2-2	2-3	4-2
Histon	2-3	2-3	2-2	1-3	0-0	1-1	5-5	3-0	1-4	1-1	4-3	2-2	4-0	2-3		1-1	1-1	3-0	0-1	3-3	1-5	2-0
Hyde	2-1	5-0	1-0	4-1	3-2	2-2	4-0	4-1	1-1	3-1	0-0	0-1	3-2	4-0	4-0		1-1	3-0	1-1	4-2	2-1	4-0
Nuneaton Town	2-1	2-0	2-2	2-0	1-1	2-0	2-1	4-0	1-0	0-0	1-1	2-0	2-5	3-2	2-0			0-1	1-2	2-1	3-0	2-1
Solihull Moors	2-0	3-1	2-2	1-0	1-0	1-2	0-2	0-2	1-2	5-3	1-0	5-1	1-2	0-2	1-0	0-0			1-1	2-3	0-0	2-1
Stalybridge Celtic	5-1	2-3	2-0	3-0	0-4	2-2	1-3	2-1	2-1	4-0	2-2	0-3	3-2	4-2	2-0	1-3	4-1	2-0		4-2	2-0	1-3
Vauxhall Motors	2-2	4-3	2-1	0-4	1-0	2-1	1-1	1-2	3-1	0-2	1-1	0-1	1-2	1-1	0-2	1-2	2-1	1-0			3-2	0-1
Worcester City	3-0	2-1	2-1	3-0	0-1	0-2	0-2	1-0	1-1	2-1			2-2	3-2	1-1	1-1	2-2	1-3	0-0	2-0		0-1
Workington	1-2	1-1	2-0	1-2	3-1	1-1	3-1	3-0	1-2	0-2	3-0	1-3	2-1	3-1	0-0	1-2	1-1	1-1	2-5	2-1	0-0	

Blue Square North (Football Conference)

Season 2011/2012

Team	P	W	D	L	F	A	Pts
Hyde	42	27	9	6	90	36	90
Guiseley	42	25	10	7	87	50	85
FC Halifax Town	42	21	11	10	80	59	74
Gainsborough Trinity	42	23	5	14	74	61	74
Nuneaton Town	42	22	12	8	74	41	72
Stalybridge Celtic	42	20	11	11	83	64	71
Worcester City	42	18	11	13	63	58	65
Altrincham	42	17	10	15	90	71	61
Droylsden	42	16	11	15	83	86	59
Bishop's Stortford	42	17	7	18	70	75	58
Boston United	42	15	9	18	60	67	54
Colwyn Bay	42	15	8	19	55	71	53
Workington	42	14	10	18	56	61	52
Gloucester City	42	15	7	20	53	60	52
Harrogate Town	42	14	10	18	59	69	52
Histon	42	12	15	15	67	72	51
Corby Town	42	14	8	20	69	71	50
Vauxhall Motors	42	14	8	20	63	78	50
Solihull Moors	42	13	10	19	44	54	49
Hinckley United	42	13	9	20	75	90	48
Blyth Spartans	42	7	13	22	50	80	34
Eastwood Town	42	4	8	30	37	105	20

Nuneaton Town had 6 points deducted for fielding an ineligible player.

Promotion Play-offs North

Gainsborough Trinity 2   FC Halifax Town 2
Nuneaton Town 1   Guiseley 1

FC Halifax Town 0   Gainsborough Trinity 1
Gainsborough Trinity won 3-2 on aggregate
Guiseley 0   Nuneaton Town .... 1 (aet.)
Nuneaton Town won 2-1 on aggregate

Gainsborough Trinity 0   Nuneaton Town 1

Promoted: Hyde and Nuneaton Town

Relegated: Blyth Spartans and Eastwood Town

Blue Square South — Football Conference South — 2011/2012 Season

	Basingstoke Town	Boreham Wood	Bromley	Chelmsford City	Dartford	Dorchester Town	Dover Athletic	Eastbourne Borough	Eastleigh	Farnborough	Hampton & Richmond Borough	Havant & Waterlooville	Maidenhead United	Salisbury City	Staines Town	Sutton United	Thurrock	Tonbridge Angels	Truro City	Welling United	Weston-super-Mare	Woking
Basingstoke Town	■	1-1	1-0	1-1	3-2	1-0	1-1	3-0	1-0	4-3	2-2	3-2	1-3	2-2	1-1	1-2	3-1	0-2	2-1	0-1	4-1	0-3
Boreham Wood	1-1	■	2-1	1-3	3-1	2-2	4-2	1-1	6-1	4-0	2-1	0-1	1-0	1-1	1-2	1-1	2-1	4-2	1-2	2-1	3-0	1-2
Bromley	1-3	4-0	■	1-0	1-2	0-0	0-1	1-3	0-0	1-1	1-2	0-0	0-1	2-2	1-1	3-0	0-0	2-2	1-1	1-1	1-0	2-4
Chelmsford City	0-1	0-0	6-1	■	0-0	0-0	2-3	1-0	3-0	2-2	1-0	3-1	2-0	2-3	0-1	2-3	1-0	2-2	0-1	1-2	3-2	2-3
Dartford	4-1	2-2	3-1	0-0	■	1-1	3-1	2-1	3-0	3-0	2-1	3-1	2-1	2-0	2-1	6-1	6-0	3-1	1-2	1-0	1-1	2-3
Dorchester Town	2-1	0-1	1-1	1-2	1-0	■	1-1	0-3	1-3	3-3	1-0	3-6	4-0	0-3	0-3	0-0	3-0	3-1	2-3	3-2	1-3	0-0
Dover Athletic	0-0	0-2	4-1	2-1	2-2	4-0	■	1-1	2-0	0-0	0-1	1-1	2-2	1-1	0-4	0-2	3-1	0-0	3-1	0-1	1-0	0-3
Eastbourne Borough	0-2	3-2	5-0	1-3	0-1	1-4	2-2	■	3-0	1-1	2-0	2-1	0-2	1-3	0-1	0-0	2-1	1-2	2-2	0-3	1-2	2-1
Eastleigh	0-2	2-0	0-2	1-1	2-2	0-1	2-3	2-1	■	0-1	1-1	3-2	4-1	1-1	2-1	4-0	3-2	1-2	3-1	3-0	2-1	0-0
Farnborough	1-0	4-0	2-1	1-3	1-2	1-2	0-2	1-0	1-3	■	0-2	1-0	0-3	1-0	1-0	0-3	0-2	3-2	2-1	1-4	0-1	0-1
Hampton & Richmond Borough	0-2	0-1	1-2	0-4	1-3	0-2	2-2	3-1	0-4	1-0	■	3-3	0-0	1-2	1-2	0-0	0-2	1-1	4-3	0-2	3-1	1-1
Havant & Waterlooville	0-1	2-4	1-2	2-3	0-4	4-2	0-1	0-0	0-0	5-0	2-2	■	2-1	2-1	3-2	2-2	3-0	1-1	4-1	1-2	1-1	3-4
Maidenhead United	1-1	0-3	3-3	1-1	1-1	0-1	1-4	1-0	4-3	3-4	0-2	2-0	■	0-1	1-1	1-1	4-0	0-4	1-3	0-4	1-3	0-1
Salisbury City	1-1	0-2	0-2	0-1	1-2	0-1	0-1	3-0	2-0	1-3	4-2	4-1	0-2	■	1-0	3-1	1-1	2-0	2-1	0-0	0-0	2-0
Staines Town	0-2	2-1	4-1	1-1	1-4	0-2	0-3	1-2	2-2	1-2	1-4	1-1	0-0	0-1	■	1-4	2-3	1-1	1-1	4-2	2-1	0-1
Sutton United	1-0	2-1	1-1	3-2	0-1	3-1	0-0	1-1	2-0	2-0	2-2	2-0	4-1	5-0	1-0	■	1-1	0-1	2-2	4-3	3-2	0-5
Thurrock	1-2	1-0	1-1	0-2	0-3	2-0	0-4	1-4	1-3	0-1	0-2	0-0	1-1	1-1	1-2	0-1	■	0-0	1-1	1-4	0-3	1-1
Tonbridge Angels	2-3	1-1	1-1	0-0	0-1	2-1	2-3	5-1	4-0	1-5	1-0	1-2	1-0	3-1	3-2	1-4	3-2	■	3-0	1-1	3-0	3-6
Truro City	2-5	2-1	1-2	0-2	1-1	1-0	0-2	2-1	8-2	3-3	0-1	1-2	2-2	2-1	0-3	3-0	2-0		■	2-3	0-1	1-4
Welling United	1-1	2-0	2-1	1-1	1-1	3-2	0-0	3-0	0-1	1-0	2-1	3-1	4-0	4-3	1-1	0-0	1-0	3-2	5-1	■	2-0	3-2
Weston-super-Mare	2-1	4-1	0-3	1-2	0-4	0-4	1-1	3-3	0-0	5-2	1-2	3-1	4-2	2-0	2-1	0-0	2-2	2-2	0-1	2-0	■	0-3
Woking	1-0	0-0	3-2	1-1	1-0	4-1	3-1	3-1	1-0	1-0	2-1	3-0	0-2	0-0	0-1	4-1	5-1	2-1	3-3	2-1	4-1	■

Blue Square South (Football Conference)

Season 2011/2012

	P	W	D	L	F	A	Pts
Woking	42	30	7	5	92	41	97
Dartford	42	26	10	6	89	40	88
Welling United	42	24	9	9	79	47	81
Sutton United	42	20	14	8	68	53	74
Basingstoke Town	42	20	11	11	65	50	71
Chelmsford City	42	18	13	11	67	44	67
Dover Athletic	42	17	15	10	62	49	66
Boreham Wood	42	17	10	15	66	58	61
Tonbridge Angels	42	15	12	15	70	67	57
Salisbury City	42	15	12	15	55	54	57
Dorchester Town	42	16	8	18	58	65	56
Eastleigh	42	15	9	18	57	63	54
Weston-super-Mare	42	14	9	19	58	71	51
Truro City	42	13	9	20	65	80	48
Staines Town	42	12	10	20	53	64	46
Farnborough	42	15	6	21	52	79	46
Bromley	42	10	15	17	52	66	45
Eastbourne Borough	42	12	9	21	54	69	45
Havant & Waterlooville	42	11	11	20	64	75	44
Maidenhead United	42	11	10	21	49	74	43
Hampton & Richmond	42	10	12	20	53	69	42
Thurrock	42	5	11	26	33	84	26

Farnborough had 5 points deducted for a breach of the League's financial rules.

Promotion Play-offs South

Basingstoke Town 0   Dartford 1
Sutton United 1   Welling United 2

Dartford 2   Basingstoke Town 1
Dartford won 3-1 on aggregate

Welling United 0   Sutton United 0
Welling United won 2-1 on aggregate

Dartford 1   Welling United 0

Promoted: Woking and Dartford

Relegated: Hampton & Richmond Borough and Thurrock

The Evo-Stik League Northern Premier League Premier Division 2011/2012 Season	Ashton United	Bradford Park Avenue	Burscough	Buxton	Chasetown	Chester	Chorley	FC United of Manchester	Frickley Athletic	Hednesford United	Kendal Town	Marine	Matlock Town	Mickleover Sports	Nantwich Town	North Ferriby United	Northwich Victoria	Rushall Olympic	Stafford Rangers	Stocksbridge Park Steels	Whitby Town	Worksop Town
Ashton United		0-1	3-2	4-2	4-0	0-2	3-1	1-0	2-0	1-2	1-0	1-2	3-0	0-3	1-1	0-1	0-3	3-1	1-5	1-2	1-2	4-2
Bradford Park Avenue	4-0		3-0	3-1	2-1	2-1	1-0	2-5	3-0	0-1	4-1	0-1	2-2	3-1	3-1	1-0	1-2	0-2	3-1	2-0	3-0	1-0
Burscough	2-3	1-1		1-2	4-4	1-4	1-4	3-5	1-3	0-4	2-2	0-4	1-2	1-3	2-1	1-2	1-3	2-4	2-3	1-1	0-1	0-2
Buxton	2-1	1-3	2-2		0-0	1-1	1-3	0-4	3-0	1-3	5-3	0-4	2-1	2-0	4-3	1-3	2-3	1-2	3-1	1-4	0-1	1-3
Chasetown	1-0	0-4	4-1	1-3		1-1	1-1	0-3	2-1	1-2	2-1	0-1	1-1	0-1	4-4	2-2	0-1	0-2	0-1	1-3	1-1	1-2
Chester	1-0	3-2	4-0	4-0	1-0		3-0	2-1	2-2	1-2	4-0	4-0	4-0	2-1	1-1	6-0	1-1	1-1	2-0	5-1	2-0	2-0
Chorley	2-2	3-1	2-1	1-0	3-2	0-2		2-0	6-0	5-1	2-3	1-2	1-0	1-0	1-0	2-0	0-0	1-0	2-2	0-0	2-2	4-1
F.C. United of Manchester	2-1	5-2	1-1	1-2	1-2	2-3	0-0		2-2	2-0	1-0	1-1	2-1	4-0	1-3	6-3	4-1	0-0	1-2	3-0	3-0	3-1
Frickley Athletic	0-1	1-2	2-0	1-1	0-1	1-3	2-1	1-3		1-1	2-1	0-1	0-2	1-2	1-2	1-0	0-0	0-0	4-3	2-0	1-2	2-1
Hednesford Town	0-0	1-1	4-0	3-2	0-1	1-0	2-0	1-2	1-0		2-3	1-1	1-1	6-1	0-0	0-0	0-2	4-1	5-4	1-1	3-1	0-0
Kendal Town	1-3	1-1	3-4	0-0	1-4	0-3	1-2	3-1	1-1	2-1		3-3	2-1	3-3	4-1	2-3	4-1	1-3	0-1	4-2	2-1	3-0
Marine	1-0	0-2	0-0	1-0	2-3	1-2	2-4	1-2	2-1	1-0	1-1		2-2	2-3	0-0	0-2	0-2	0-3	0-1	1-0	1-2	4-0
Matlock Town	0-2	0-1	3-1	1-1	2-2	0-1	4-0	2-1	3-0	1-2	1-0	1-1		2-1	1-0	3-0	1-0	1-0	1-1	4-0	2-4	1-1
Mickleover Sports	1-1	4-0	1-1	1-3	2-3	1-3	3-4	0-2	3-6	1-2	0-6	0-1	3-1		3-1	4-0	0-2	2-2	1-0	1-3	5-0	1-1
Nantwich Town	1-1	0-3	3-4	0-0	0-0	4-1	1-0	1-1	0-0	2-2	3-0	1-2	2-1	1-1		2-1	3-2	4-1	2-0	1-0	2-0	0-1
North Ferriby United	6-3	2-1	0-0	1-4	1-1	0-3	1-2	0-0	1-2	1-2	4-2	2-0	1-1	3-1	3-1		2-3	1-0	3-1	2-1	1-0	0-0
Northwich Victoria	3-1	1-0	2-1	1-1	3-1	1-1	1-3	2-1	2-2	1-2	2-0	1-0	0-0	3-1	2-1	2-0		2-0	0-1	2-0	2-0	2-1
Rushall Olympic	1-0	0-0	3-0	3-1	1-0	0-4	1-0	1-0	1-2	2-1	2-3	0-1	1-0	1-1	0-1	1-1	0-3		2-1	3-0	3-2	0-0
Stafford Rangers	1-2	3-1	1-1	0-2	4-1	0-3	0-1	0-2	2-0	0-1	1-2	2-1	1-1	1-1	1-1	1-1	1-1	1-1		5-1	3-3	2-2
Stocksbridge Park Steels	1-1	2-2	0-2	0-1	2-0	1-2	0-3	2-2	1-1	4-0	1-3	1-1	1-1	1-5	7-0	3-4	2-0	1-0			0-2	3-0
Whitby Town	2-2	1-4	3-3	3-4	2-0	0-4	0-1	0-0	1-1	0-2	1-1	1-2	1-1	1-1	4-5	0-2	2-1	2-1	2-1	3-3		3-4
Worksop Town	3-3	0-2	2-3	2-1	4-1	0-3	1-5	2-3	2-1	1-0	3-5	0-3	2-0	5-4	3-0	0-0	0-1	2-1	1-1	1-1	0-1	

Evo-Stik League Premier Division

Season 2011/2012

Chester	42	31	7	4	102	29	100
Northwich Victoria	42	26	8	8	73	43	83
Chorley	42	24	7	11	76	48	79
Bradford Park Avenue	42	24	6	12	77	49	78
Hednesford Town	42	21	10	11	67	49	73
FC United of Manchester	42	21	9	12	83	51	72
Marine	42	19	9	14	56	50	66
Rushall Olympic	42	17	10	15	52	51	61
North Ferriby United	42	16	10	16	56	70	58
Nantwich Town	42	15	13	14	65	61	57
Kendal Town	42	15	8	19	78	83	53
Ashton United	42	15	8	19	61	67	53
Buxton	42	15	8	19	64	77	53
Matlock Town	42	12	14	16	52	54	50
Worksop Town	42	13	10	19	56	76	49
Stafford Rangers	42	12	12	18	60	65	48
Whitby Town	42	12	11	19	57	80	47
Stocksbridge Park Steels	42	10	12	20	57	75	42
Frickley Athletic	42	10	12	20	48	69	42
Chasetown	42	10	11	21	50	75	41
Mickleover Sports	42	11	10	21	67	85	40
Burscough	42	5	11	26	54	104	26

Mickleover Sports had 3 points deducted for fielding an ineligible player.

Nantwich Town had 1 point deducted for fielding an ineligible player.

Northwich Victoria had 3 points deducted for fielding an ineligible player and were later expelled from the Northern Premier League after being found guilty of failing to comply with the League's financial rules.

On appeal this punishment was reduced to relegation from the League's Premier Division.

Promotion Play-offs

Chorley 0   FC United of Manchester 2
Bradford Park Avenue 5   Hednesford Town 0

Bradford Park Avenue 1   FC Utd. of Manchester 0 (aet.)

Promoted: Chester and Bradford Park Avenue

Relegated: Northwich Victoria, Chasetown, Mickleover Sports and Burscough

The Evo-Stik League Southern Premier Division 2011/2012 Season

	AFC Totton	Arlesey Town	Banbury United	Barwell	Bashley	Bedford Town	Brackley Town	Cambridge City	Chesham United	Chippenham Town	Cirencester Town	Evesham United	Frome Town	Hemel Hempstead Town	Hitchin Town	Leamington	Oxford City	Redditch United	St. Albans City	Stourbridge	Swindon Supermarine	Weymouth
AFC Totton		6-0	2-1	2-1	2-0	2-0	2-2	2-3	3-0	1-1	3-0	3-1	1-1	2-0	0-1	1-1	6-0	0-0	1-1	1-0	4-0	2-0
Arlesey Town	0-2		2-1	1-2	0-2	1-0	2-0	0-1	2-4	1-1	0-1	1-0	0-1	3-0	0-0	0-2	1-4	0-3	1-1	1-1	1-1	3-1
Banbury United	0-1	1-2		3-0	4-0	1-2	0-2	2-0	1-2	1-1	2-1	1-2	2-2	0-0	1-1	1-1	1-0	2-0	4-1	1-1	1-1	1-5
Barwell	3-2	1-1	3-1		2-3	1-1	5-4	0-2	2-0	5-3	1-1	1-1	3-1	2-3	2-1	3-1	0-2	1-1	0-1	2-2	2-0	1-0
Bashley	4-4	0-0	0-3	0-2		3-3	1-1	0-1	3-1	0-0	2-3	0-0	1-1	2-0	1-3	2-1	0-2	2-1	4-1	1-0	3-3	3-3
Bedford Town	1-2	0-2	1-0	3-2	2-2		5-2	1-2	0-4	1-0	1-1	3-1	0-1	0-1	1-3	1-2	1-2	0-1	2-2	2-2	3-0	2-1
Brackley Town	0-3	2-1	1-1	2-1	3-2	7-1		4-2	3-2	5-1	0-0	2-0	1-1	3-0	3-0	3-0	5-2	2-0	6-0	0-2	4-0	3-1
Cambridge City	1-0	3-1	3-0	2-1	4-0	6-1	2-3		2-2	3-0	3-1	1-2	2-3	3-0	3-1	2-2	2-0	1-1	4-0	0-0	1-1	3-0
Chesham United	2-1	2-0	3-0	1-0	2-1	3-4	2-3	1-0		1-2	2-1	2-1	2-0	2-1	2-0	1-1	1-1	1-0	2-2	4-2	2-1	4-1
Chippenham Town	2-1	1-1	1-1	0-3	1-3	3-0	0-1	2-2	1-0		0-1	1-0	1-1	4-1	0-1	1-2	0-1	2-0	4-0	1-2	0-2	3-0
Cirencester Town	1-2	0-3	1-3	2-2	0-1	2-4	0-2	0-2	1-1	0-1		1-2	0-1	0-0	2-2	2-1	0-1	0-2	1-2	1-3	0-1	0-1
Evesham United	1-0	1-3	2-5	1-3	0-1	0-0	0-2	2-1	0-2	2-4	2-3		1-0	2-2	1-1	1-2	0-1	1-1	1-1	0-1	3-4	4-0
Frome Town	1-3	2-2	0-1	1-0	1-1	0-0	1-1	1-1	0-1	0-2	1-0	1-2		1-1	0-0	0-0	0-3	3-2	0-1	1-1	2-0	0-0
Hemel Hempstead Town	0-3	1-1	2-1	2-3	2-2	1-1	1-1	1-2	1-1	1-1	4-1	2-3	3-1		2-0	1-1	2-0	0-2	0-4	2-0	0-0	1-2
Hitchin Town	2-2	2-0	1-2	0-0	2-3	1-3	2-1	3-2	1-1	2-0	6-2	0-1	1-3	3-0		0-0	0-3	2-1	0-3	2-0	0-1	3-1
Leamington	2-1	1-0	3-1	3-0	1-0	0-4	0-0	4-2	3-2	0-0	2-0	1-1	1-1	3-1	1-0		1-1	1-2	1-0	4-2	2-2	4-1
Oxford City	2-2	3-0	0-1	2-0	3-0	1-0	1-1	0-0	2-0	2-1	0-0	2-0	2-0	1-1	0-0	2-1		1-1	3-1	1-2	7-1	2-0
Redditch United	0-0	0-1	1-0	2-0	2-2	2-0	2-3	2-0	1-1	0-2	3-1	0-4	1-0	1-4	1-1	1-1	1-1		3-4	0-1	0-1	2-2
St. Albans City	3-4	2-2	1-1	1-6	2-0	1-2	1-1	3-0	1-1	1-4	4-1	4-1	2-1	2-1	4-4	2-1	3-2	2-0		2-1	2-1	2-2
Stourbridge	2-1	2-0	5-0	1-1	5-0	1-1	1-0	1-1	2-1	3-1	2-1	3-1	4-0	1-0	0-0	0-0	2-0	1-0	2-1		4-1	1-2
Swindon Supermarine	0-0	2-1	2-0	0-2	1-2	0-1	0-2	3-1	0-6	0-4	4-4	2-2	0-2	1-3	2-1	0-1	2-4	0-2	2-1	2-1		2-2
Weymouth	3-1	0-2	2-1	1-1	2-1	0-2	0-1	1-2	2-2	2-0	3-1	2-2	0-3	0-1	2-1	2-1	1-0	2-3	3-1	1-1	2-2	

The Evo-Stik League Southern Premier Division

Season 2011/2012

Brackley Town	42	25	10	7	92	48	85
Oxford City	42	22	11	9	68	41	77
AFC Totton	42	21	11	10	81	43	74
Chesham United	42	21	10	11	76	53	73
Cambridge City	42	21	9	12	78	52	72
Stourbridge	42	20	12	10	67	45	72
Leamington	42	18	15	9	60	47	69
St Albans City	42	17	11	14	72	77	62
Barwell	42	17	10	15	70	61	61
Bedford Town	42	15	10	17	60	69	55
Chippenham Town	42	14	11	17	55	53	53
Frome Town	42	12	16	14	44	49	52
Bashley	42	13	13	16	58	74	52
Hitchin Town	42	13	12	17	54	57	51
Redditch United	42	14	9	19	45	50	51
Banbury United	42	13	10	19	54	61	49
Weymouth	42	13	9	20	54	75	48
Arlesey Town	42	12	11	19	43	60	47
Hemel Hempstead Town	42	10	14	18	46	66	44
Evesham United	42	12	8	22	49	71	44
Swindon Supermarine	42	11	11	20	50	86	44
Cirencester Town	42	7	9	26	40	78	30

Promotion Play-offs

Oxford City 1   Cambrdige City 0
AFC Totton 3   Chesham United 2

Oxford City 4   AFC Totton 2

Promoted: Brackley Town and Oxford City

Relegated: Evesham United, Swindon Supermarine and Cirencester Town

Ryman Football League Premier Division 2011/2012 Season	Billericay Town	AFC Hornchurch	Lowestoft Town	Wealdstone	Bury Town	Lewes	Hendon	Canvey Island	Cray Wanderers	East Thurrock United	Kingstonian	Metropolitan Police	Wingate & Finchley	Concord Rangers	Margate	Carshalton Athletic	Harrow Borough	Hastings United	Leatherhead	Aveley	Tooting & Mitcham United	Horsham
Billericay Town	■	0-1	1-4	0-0	4-4	1-0	2-1	4-2	3-1	1-0	6-0	2-1	2-0	0-0	1-1	1-1	3-0	2-0	2-1	2-1	5-1	2-2
AFC Hornchurch	0-0	■	3-0	1-1	0-1	1-0	0-1	1-2	1-2	1-0	3-0	1-0	1-0	2-0	3-0	1-1	0-0	0-1	2-1	2-1	6-0	0-2
Lowestoft Town	1-0	2-1	■	2-1	2-1	3-1	2-0	1-1	2-1	1-1	3-2	2-2	2-0	5-0	2-1	3-2	1-2	1-3	2-2	1-0	2-2	1-0
Wealdstone	1-1	2-1	0-0	■	3-1	1-0	0-2	1-2	1-1	2-2	4-1	1-0	2-4	3-1	1-1	1-1	4-0	2-1	1-0	5-2	2-0	3-0
Bury Town	1-1	2-1	2-3	1-1	■	2-1	0-1	2-0	1-1	5-2	1-1	0-1	2-2	2-0	2-1	2-0	2-2	5-0	2-1	1-0	4-2	3-0
Lewes	2-1	0-4	2-2	1-0	1-1	■	3-2	1-2	1-0	2-2	1-1	1-0	0-0	1-2	2-0	1-0	4-2	2-1	1-0	4-1	3-1	1-1
Hendon	1-2	2-0	1-0	1-1	3-4	2-2	■	1-0	1-0	1-1	2-1	1-3	1-1	1-0	0-3	1-1	3-2	2-1	1-2	1-1	5-0	1-1
Canvey Island	0-2	4-1	3-2	3-1	0-1	1-2	3-1	■	1-2	1-0	0-2	2-2	2-3	0-2	5-0	1-2	1-0	1-2	3-1	0-3	2-0	1-0
Cray Wanderers	2-3	2-5	0-2	2-1	2-0	0-1	0-0	0-0	■	3-0	0-0	2-1	3-2	2-4	2-4	1-0	1-2	1-0	1-2	2-2	4-1	3-1
East Thurrock United	1-2	0-1	1-3	3-3	2-1	1-0	0-0	2-1	1-2	■	0-1	4-2	1-2	4-1	3-0	1-1	0-3	0-2	3-0	4-1	1-0	1-0
Kingstonian	0-2	0-2	2-0	0-3	1-1	1-0	1-0	1-2	4-2	2-5	■	2-1	2-2	0-1	2-1	2-3	1-0	1-1	0-3	2-0	2-1	3-4
Metropolitan Police	0-1	0-2	0-2	1-2	0-1	0-0	0-1	3-1	1-0	1-2	2-1	■	2-0	3-0	1-3	5-0	1-0	4-0	2-1	0-0	3-0	4-1
Wingate & Finchley	1-4	1-2	2-1	0-5	3-2	1-2	0-5	0-2	0-2	3-3	0-2	2-1	■	3-1	2-2	2-1	2-2	3-1	1-0	2-2	4-2	3-2
Concord Rangers	0-0	1-2	3-2	1-2	4-2	2-3	2-0	1-2	1-1	4-5	2-3	0-3	1-1	■	1-1	0-0	1-0	2-2	2-1	3-0	3-4	5-0
Margate	2-2	0-2	1-4	0-2	2-3	5-1	0-2	1-1	1-3	5-0	2-1	1-3	5-0	1-0	■	0-1	1-0	4-1	0-0	3-0	1-2	2-1
Carshalton Athletic	0-1	1-2	1-4	0-0	2-1	1-2	0-3	0-1	2-3	0-1	0-1	2-1	3-0	0-2	2-1	■	0-1	2-0	1-1	0-0	3-0	2-1
Harrow Borough	1-1	1-0	2-4	0-0	2-1	0-1	4-2	3-4	0-4	3-1	1-3	1-3	0-3	0-2	1-2	1-2	■	1-1	2-0	1-1	1-1	2-0
Hastings United	0-0	1-3	2-0	0-2	0-1	0-1	0-2	1-1	0-2	1-2	1-0	0-2	0-1	1-1	2-2	0-2	3-1	■	0-0	2-1	2-0	5-0
Leatherhead	0-2	0-1	1-2	1-1	0-5	0-1	0-1	0-1	1-4	2-1	0-2	1-1	2-2	1-3	2-0	0-1	2-0	2-0	■	2-0	2-4	2-1
Aveley	0-6	2-3	0-1	0-3	1-2	0-0	1-7	2-4	1-1	0-3	0-0	0-1	1-2	3-3	1-3	1-1	3-2	0-1	1-1	■	1-3	2-1
Tooting & Mitcham United	4-2	1-2	2-1	0-6	1-7	2-2	0-3	0-1	0-4	0-1	1-4	0-1	1-1	0-6	1-1	4-3	1-3	1-2	1-4	1-2	■	2-2
Horsham	0-5	0-3	1-2	1-1	1-3	0-1	0-3	1-2	1-5	1-5	1-3	2-2	1-2	0-3	1-2	1-3	1-3	1-2	1-4	1-3	2-0	■

Ryman League Premier Division

Season 2011/2012

Billericay Town	42	24	13	5	82	38	85
AFC Hornchurch	42	26	4	12	68	35	82
Lowestoft Town	42	25	7	10	80	53	82
Wealdstone	42	20	15	7	76	39	75
Bury Town	42	22	9	11	85	55	75
Lewes	42	21	10	11	55	47	73
Hendon	42	21	9	12	69	44	72
Canvey Island	42	22	5	15	66	55	71
Cray Wanderers	42	20	8	14	74	55	68
East Thurrock United	42	18	8	16	70	65	62
Kingstonian	42	18	7	17	58	64	61
Metropolitan Police	42	18	6	18	63	46	60
Wingate & Finchley	42	16	11	15	63	79	59
Concord Rangers	42	16	9	17	72	66	57
Margate	42	15	9	18	66	65	54
Carshalton Athletic	42	14	10	18	48	55	52
Harrow Borough	42	13	8	21	53	70	47
Hastings United	42	13	8	21	43	61	47
Leatherhead	42	11	8	23	46	62	41
Aveley	42	5	12	25	41	88	27
Tooting & Mitcham United	42	7	6	29	47	116	27
Horsham	42	3	6	33	38	105	14

Horsham had 1 point deducted for fielding an ineligible player.

Promotion Play-offs

AFC Hornchurch 1   Bury Town 1
Lowestoft Town 2   Wealdstone 1

AFC Hornchurch 2   Lowestoft Town .... 1 (aet.)

Promoted: Billericay Town and AFC Hornchurch

Relegated: Leatherhead, Aveley, Tooting & Mitcham United and Horsham

F.A. Trophy 2011/2012

Qualifying 1	Arlesey Town	3	AFC Sudbury	1
Qualifying 1	Aveley	0	Bury Town	1
Qualifying 1	Aylesbury	0	Tiverton Town	0
Qualifying 1	Barton Rovers	0	Belper Town	1
Qualifying 1	Bashley	2	Worthing	2
Qualifying 1	Bedfont Town	1	Hastings United	1
Qualifying 1	Bedworth United	0	Hednesford Town	1
Qualifying 1	Billericay Town	1	Whitehawk	0
Qualifying 1	Brackley Town	1	Mickleover Sports	0
Qualifying 1	Bradford Park Avenue	1	Worksop Town	1
Qualifying 1	Brentwood Town	2	Lowestoft Town	3
Qualifying 1	Burscough	0	Salford City	1
Qualifying 1	Buxton	4	Garforth Town	2
Qualifying 1	Canvey Island	4	Hendon	0
Qualifying 1	Carshalton Athletic	3	Bideford	1
Qualifying 1	Chasetown	5	Grantham Town	0
Qualifying 1	Chertsey Town	2	Chalfont St Peter	0
Qualifying 1	Chesham United	5	Horsham	0
Qualifying 1	Chester FC	2	Ashton United	1
Qualifying 1	Chipstead	1	Margate	3
Qualifying 1	Cirencester Town	3	Leatherhead	1
Qualifying 1	Concord Rangers	2	Harlow Town	3
Qualifying 1	Daventry Town	4	Kidsgrove Athletic	3
Qualifying 1	Dulwich Hamlet	0	Harrow Borough	2
Qualifying 1	East Thurrock United	1	Bedford Town	1
Qualifying 1	Eastbourne Town	1	Hitchin Town	3
Qualifying 1	Evesham United	1	Barwell	1
Qualifying 1	Farsley	2	Curzon Ashton	2
Qualifying 1	Fleet Town	0	Yate Town	5
Qualifying 1	Folkestone Invicta	1	Metropolitan Police	0
Qualifying 1	Frickley Athletic	0	FC United of Manchester	4
Qualifying 1	Frome Town	0	Thatcham Town	1
Qualifying 1	Goole AFC	2	Durham City	3
Qualifying 1	Gosport Borough	1	Sholing	0
Qualifying 1	Hemel Hempstead Town	1	Croydon Athletic	1
Qualifying 1	Hythe Town	1	Burgess Hill Town	0
Qualifying 1	Ilkeston FC	2	Biggleswade Town	0
Qualifying 1	Kendal Town	1	Nantwich Town	0
Qualifying 1	Kingstonian	0	Godalming Town	1
Qualifying 1	Leek Town	4	Hucknall Town	1
Qualifying 1	Leighton Town	0	Banbury United	1
Qualifying 1	Lewes	2	Cray Wanderers	1
Qualifying 1	Marine	1	Chorley	0
Qualifying 1	Marlow	1	Didcot Town	1
Qualifying 1	Matlock Town	3	Stamford	0
Qualifying 1	Merstham	0	Maldon & Tiptree	4
Qualifying 1	Newcastle Town	1	Stafford Rangers	1
Qualifying 1	North Ferriby United	3	Lincoln United	1
Qualifying 1	Northwich Victoria	4	AFC Fylde	2
Qualifying 1	Oxford City	0	Mangotsfield United	3
Qualifying 1	Poole Town	1	Chippenham Town	1
Qualifying 1	Potters Bar Town	1	AFC Hayes	0
Qualifying 1	Radcliffe Borough	2	Harrogate Railway Athletic	1
Qualifying 1	Redbridge	3	Needham Market	1

Qualifying 1	Romulus	1	Leamington	0
Qualifying 1	Rushall Olympic	0	Cambridge City	2
Qualifying 1	Sheffield	3	Bamber Bridge	0
Qualifying 1	St Albans City	1	Ashford Town (Middlesex)	3
Qualifying 1	St Neots Town	3	Sutton Coldfield Town	1
Qualifying 1	Stocksbridge Park Steels	2	Ossett Town	2
Qualifying 1	Stourbridge	2	Redditch United	1
Qualifying 1	Swindon Supermarine	–	Andover	–
	Swindon Supermarine progressed to the next round after Andover folded			
Qualifying 1	Taunton Town	0	Paulton Rovers	3
Qualifying 1	Thamesmead Town	2	Enfield Town	0
Qualifying 1	Uxbridge	3	Sittingbourne	1
Qualifying 1	Waltham Forest	0	Faversham Town	1
Qualifying 1	Wealdstone	3	Tooting & Mitcham United	0
Qualifying 1	Weymouth	3	AFC Totton	2
Qualifying 1	Whyteleafe	0	Grays Athletic	3
Qualifying 1	Wingate & Finchley	1	AFC Hornchurch	2
Qualifying 1	Witton Albion	6	Brigg Town	1
Qualifying 1	Woodley Sports	3	Whitby Town	1
Replay	Barwell	5	Evesham United	1
Replay	Bedford Town	1	East Thurrock United	2
Replay	Chippenham Town	2	Poole Town	1
Replay	Croydon Athletic	0	Hemel Hempstead Town	2
Replay	Curzon Ashton	2	Farsley	0
Replay	Didcot Town	4	Marlow	0
Replay	Hastings United	0	Bedfont Town	2
Replay	Ossett Town	3	Stocksbridge Park Steels	2
Replay	Stafford Rangers	5	Newcastle Town	2
Replay	Tiverton Town	2	Aylesbury	1
Replay	Worksop Town	4	Bradford Park Avenue	1
Replay	Worthing	4	Bashley	2 (aet)
Qualifying 2	Banbury United	3	Paulton Rovers	1
Qualifying 2	Billericay Town	2	St Neots Town	0
Qualifying 2	Bury Town	3	Hythe Town	2
Qualifying 2	Cambridge City	1	Redbridge	2
Qualifying 2	Carshalton Athletic	3	Cirencester Town	1
Qualifying 2	Chertsey Town	6	Ashford Town (Middlesex)	5
Qualifying 2	Chesham United	2	Tiverton Town	2
Qualifying 2	Chester FC	2	Stafford Rangers	0
Qualifying 2	Chippenham Town	1	Mangotsfield United	1
Qualifying 2	Curzon Ashton	2	Belper Town	1
Qualifying 2	Durham City	1	FC United of Manchester	1
Qualifying 2	Faversham Town	2	East Thurrock United	4
Qualifying 2	Folkestone Invicta	4	Daventry Town	2
Qualifying 2	Gosport Borough	4	Godalming Town	0
Qualifying 2	Grays Athletic	2	Canvey Island	3
Qualifying 2	Harlow Town	3	Lewes	2
Qualifying 2	Harrow Borough	1	AFC Hornchurch	1
Qualifying 2	Hednesford Town	0	Matlock Town	0
Qualifying 2	Hemel Hempstead Town	2	Brackley Town	3
Qualifying 2	Hitchin Town	1	Lowestoft Town	3
Qualifying 2	Ilkeston FC	2	Woodley Sports	1
Qualifying 2	Leek Town	3	Witton Albion	3
Qualifying 2	Maldon & Tiptree	3	Bedfont Town	2
Qualifying 2	Margate	1	Wealdstone	1
Qualifying 2	Marine	5	Chasetown	2

Qualifying 2	North Ferriby United	3	Salford City	0	
Qualifying 2	Northwich Victoria	3	Buxton	0	
Qualifying 2	Ossett Town	4	Barwell	2	
Qualifying 2	Radcliffe Borough	1	Worksop Town	1	
Qualifying 2	Sheffield	2	Romulus	0	
Qualifying 2	Stourbridge	3	Kendal Town	3	
Qualifying 2	Thamesmead Town	3	Arlesey Town	2	
Qualifying 2	Thatcham Town	1	Weymouth	1	
Qualifying 2	Uxbridge	5	Potters Bar Town	2	
Qualifying 2	Worthing	0	Didcot Town	2	
Qualifying 2	Yate Town	0	Swindon Supermarine	1	
Replay	AFC Hornchurch	1	Harrow Borough	0	
Replay	FC United of Manchester	3	Durham City	1	(aet)
Replay	Kendal Town	0	Stourbridge	6	
Replay	Mangotsfield United	0	Chippenham Town	2	
Replay	Matlock Town	2	Hednesford Town	1	
Replay	Tiverton Town	1	Chesham United	0	
Replay	Wealdstone	2	Margate	1	
Replay	Weymouth	6	Thatcham Town	1	
Replay	Witton Albion	4	Leek Town	1	
Replay	Worksop Town	2	Radcliffe Borough	0	
Qualifying 3	Banbury United	0	Wealdstone	0	
Qualifying 3	Bishop's Stortford	1	Tonbridge Angels	1	
Qualifying 3	Blyth Spartans	1	Stalybridge Celtic	3	
Qualifying 3	Boreham Wood	1	Dover Athletic	0	
Qualifying 3	Boston United	1	Workington	0	
Qualifying 3	Brackley Town	2	Chertsey Town	0	
Qualifying 3	Bromley	1	Didcot Town	3	
Qualifying 3	Chelmsford City	2	Woking	0	
Qualifying 3	Chippenham Town	1	Eastleigh	1	
Qualifying 3	Colwyn Bay	0	FC Halifax Town	0	
Qualifying 3	Corby Town	1	North Ferriby United	1	
Qualifying 3	Dorchester Town	1	Gosport Borough	2	
Qualifying 3	Droylsden	2	Witton Albion	1	
Qualifying 3	Eastbourne Borough	0	Dartford	0	
Qualifying 3	FC United of Manchester	2	Altrincham	1	
Qualifying 3	Farnborough	2	Bury Town	2	
Qualifying 3	Folkestone Invicta	1	Staines Town	3	
Qualifying 3	Gainsborough Trinity	0	Hinckley United	1	
Qualifying 3	Gloucester City	1	Truro City	1	
Qualifying 3	Guiseley	7	Eastwood Town	0	
Qualifying 3	Hampton & Richmond Borough	4	Canvey Island	2	
Qualifying 3	Harlow Town	1	Lowestoft Town	2	
Qualifying 3	Maidenhead United	1	Billericay Town	0	
Qualifying 3	Maldon & Tiptree	0	Carshalton Athletic	1	
Qualifying 3	Matlock Town	0	Hyde	1	
Qualifying 3	Northwich Victoria	1	Ilkeston FC	1	
Qualifying 3	Redbridge	1	East Thurrock United	2	
Qualifying 3	Salisbury City	2	Weston-Super-Mare	0	
Qualifying 3	Sheffield	0	Nuneaton Town	4	
Qualifying 3	Solihull Moors	2	Ossett Town	2	
Qualifying 3	Stourbridge	0	Chester FC	2	
Qualifying 3	Sutton United	1	Basingstoke Town	2	
Qualifying 3	Thamesmead Town	2	Welling United	2	
Qualifying 3	Thurrock	0	AFC Hornchurch	5	
Qualifying 3	Tiverton Town	0	Swindon Supermarine	1	

Qualifying 3	Uxbridge	2	Histon	1	
Qualifying 3	Vauxhall Motors	3	Marine	2	
Qualifying 3	Weymouth	0	Havant & Waterlooville	0	
Qualifying 3	Worcester City	0	Harrogate Town	1	
Qualifying 3	Worksop Town	3	Curzon Ashton	2	
Replay	Bury Town	0	Farnborough	2	
Replay	Dartford	2	Eastbourne Borough	1	
Replay	Eastleigh	1	Chippenham Town	1	(aet)
	Chippenham Town won 8-7 on penalties				
Replay	FC Halifax Town	1	Colwyn Bay	2	
Replay	Havant & Waterlooville	0	Weymouth	2	
Replay	Ilkeston FC	1	Northwich Victoria	5	
Replay	North Ferriby United	3	Corby Town	2	
Replay	Ossett Town	0	Solihull Moors	1	
Replay	Tonbridge Angels	1	Bishop's Stortford	2	
Replay	Truro City	3	Gloucester City	2	
Replay	Wealdstone	4	Banbury United	0	
Replay	Welling United	3	Thamesmead Town	1	
Round 1	AFC Hornchurch	0	Farnborough	0	
Round 1	Alfreton Town	4	Southport	0	
Round 1	Barrow	3	Harrogate Town	2	
Round 1	Boreham Wood	0	Cambridge United	1	
Round 1	Boston United	2	Hyde	1	
Round 1	Brackley Town	0	Dartford	3	
Round 1	Carshalton Athletic	5	Bishop's Stortford	0	
Round 1	Chelmsford City	2	Bath City	3	
Round 1	Colwyn Bay	1	Lincoln City	3	
Round 1	Didcot Town	0	Basingstoke Town	1	
Round 1	Droylsden	2	Mansfield Town	1	
Round 1	East Thurrock United	2	Welling United	1	
Round 1	Gateshead	3	Kettering Town	2	
Round 1	Gosport Borough	0	Braintree Town	1	
Round 1	Grimsby Town	3	Darlington	0	
Round 1	Guiseley	2	FC United of Manchester	0	
Round 1	Hampton & Richmond Borough	2	Hayes & Yeading United	0	
Round 1	Luton Town	2	Swindon Supermarine	0	
Round 1	Newport County	0	Forest Green Rovers	0	
Round 1	North Ferriby United	1	Chester FC	5	
Round 1	Northwich Victoria	3	Fleetwood Town	1	
Round 1	Nuneaton Town	0	AFC Telford United	2	
Round 1	Salisbury City	4	Lowestoft Town	1	
Round 1	Staines Town	0	Maidenhead United	0	
Round 1	Stockport County	2	Stalybridge Celtic	2	
Round 1	Truro City	2	Ebbsfleet United	5	
Round 1	Vauxhall Motors	4	Kidderminster Harriers	4	
Round 1	Wealdstone	5	Uxbridge	0	
Round 1	Weymouth	2	Chippenham Town	1	
Round 1	Worksop Town	1	Tamworth	0	
Round 1	Wrexham	1	Hinckley United	2	
Round 1	York City	2	Solihull Moors	2	
Replay	Farnborough	2	AFC Hornchurch	3	
Replay	Forest Green Rovers	0	Newport County	2	
Replay	Kidderminster Harriers	2	Vauxhall Motors	0	
Replay	Maidenhead United	1	Staines Town	2	
Replay	Solihull Moors	0	York City	3	
Replay	Stalybridge Celtic	2	Stockport County	1	

Round 2	Bath City	1	Basingstoke Town	0	
Round 2	Cambridge United	4	AFC Telford United	1	
Round 2	Dartford	4	Boston United	2	
Round 2	East Thurrock United	1	Hampton & Richmond Borough	1	
Round 2	Ebbsfleet United	3	Chester FC	2	
Round 2	Gateshead	2	Braintree Town	2	
Round 2	Grimsby Town	4	AFC Hornchurch	0	
Round 2	Guiseley	2	Stalybridge Celtic	0	
Round 2	Hinckley United	0	Luton Town	0	
Round 2	Kidderminster Harriers	5	Droylsden	1	
Round 2	Lincoln City	0	Carshalton Athletic	0	
Round 2	Northwich Victoria	1	Staines Town	0	
Round 2	Salisbury City	2	York City	6	
Round 2	Wealdstone	2	Barrow	1	
Round 2	Weymouth	0	Alfreton Town	6	
Round 2	Worksop Town	1	Newport County	3	
Replay	Braintree Town	1	Gateshead	1	(aet)
	Gateshead won 4-3 on penalties				
Replay	Carshalton Athletic	3	Lincoln City	1	
Replay	Hampton & Richmond Borough	4	East Thurrock United	1	
Replay	Luton Town	3	Hinckley United	0	
Round 3	Bath City	1	Grimsby Town	2	
Round 3	Cambridge United	1	Guiseley	0	
Round 3	Dartford	2	Wealdstone	2	
Round 3	Gateshead	2	Alfreton Town	1	
Round 3	Kidderminster Harriers	1	Luton Town	2	
Round 3	Newport County	4	Carshalton Athletic	0	
Round 3	Northwich Victoria	4	Hampton & Richmond Borough	1	
Round 3	York City	1	Ebbsfleet United	0	
Replay	Wealdstone	1	Dartford	0	
Round 4	Cambridge United	1	Wealdstone	2	
Round 4	Grimsby Town	0	York City	1	
Round 4	Luton Town	2	Gateshead	0	
Round 4	Northwich Victoria	2	Newport County	3	
Semi-Finals					
1st leg	Newport County	3	Wealdstone	1	
2nd leg	Wealdstone	0	Newport County	0	
	Newport County won 3-1 on aggregate				
1st leg	York City	1	Luton Town	0	
2nd leg	Luton Town	1	York City	1	
	York City won 2-1 on aggregate				
FINAL	York City	2	Newport County	0	

F.A. Vase 2011/2012

Round 1	Alresford Town	1	Winchester City	6
Round 1	Ardley United	1	Reading Town	3
Round 1	Armthorpe Welfare	3	Yorkshire Amateur	0
Round 1	Arnold Town	0	Long Eaton United	2
Round 1	Askern Villa	3	Selby Town	1
Round 1	Atherton LR	1	Winsford United	2
Round 1	Bardon Hill Sports	2	Desborough Town	0
Round 1	Barking	0	Royston Town	1
Round 1	Bartley Green	0	Ellesmere Rangers	6
Round 1	Barton Town Old Boys	1	Pontefract Collieries	0
Round 1	Basildon United	0	Ampthill Town	4
Round 1	Bedlington Terriers	4	Sunderland RCA	1
Round 1	Bethnal Green United	3	Hoddesdon Town	1
Round 1	Billingham Town	5	South Shields	2
Round 1	Binfield	3	Hillingdon Borough	2	(aet)
Round 1	Bishop Sutton	2	Bradford Town	1
Round 1	Blackfield & Langley	2	Brockenhurst	1
Round 1	Blackwell Miners Welfare	1	Pinxton	0
Round 1	Boston Town	3	Holwell Sports	1
Round 1	Bournemouth (Ams)	2	Hartley Wintney	0
Round 1	Brading Town	4	Alton Town	5
Round 1	Brocton	3	Coventry Copsewood	0
Round 1	Burnham Ramblers	1	Sporting Bengal United	3
Round 1	Camberley Town	1	Littlehampton Town	2	(aet)
Round 1	Cheadle Town	0	Bacup Borough	2
Round 1	Christchurch	2	Bridport	1
Round 1	Cogenhoe United	2	Yaxley	1
Round 1	Continental Star	0	Gornal Athletic	2
Round 1	Cowes Sports	3	Gillingham Town	0
Round 1	Cullompton Rangers	2	Tavistock	1
Round 1	Darlington Railway Athletic (2)	1	Gillford Park	4
Round 1	Deeping Rangers	3	Holbeach United	1
Round 1	Dereham Town	0	Thetford Town	3
Round 1	Dinnington Town	0	Bridlington Town	2
Round 1	Diss Town	1	Brantham Athletic	0
Round 1	Downton	3	Fareham Town	0
Round 1	East Preston	3	Pagham	4
Round 1	Eccleshill United	1	Thackley	0
Round 1	Egham Town	3	Greenwich Borough	0
Round 1	Ellistown	0	Peterborough Northern Star	2
Round 1	Erith Town	6	Farnham Town	1
Round 1	FC Clacton	2	Whitton United	4	(aet)
Round 1	Fairford Town	0	Winterbourne United	1
Round 1	Falmouth Town	5	Buckland Athletic	2
Round 1	Felixstowe & Walton United	1	Haverhill Rovers	0
Round 1	Flackwell Heath	2	Clanfield 85	0
Round 1	Formby	0	Ashville	1
Round 1	Glasshoughton Welfare	2	AFC Emley	0
Round 1	Glossop North End	5	Blidworth Welfare	0
Round 1	Guisborough Town	4	Consett	4	(aet)
Round 1	Halstead Town	0	Team Bury	1
Round 1	Hanwell Town	1	Wantage Town	2
Round 1	Hanworth Villa	3	Bedfont Sports	1
Round 1	Harborough Town	2	Stewarts & Lloyds (2)	2	(aet)
Round 1	Haringey Borough	2	Hadley	0

Round 1	Henley Town	0	Newport Pagnell Town	1	
Round 1	Highworth Town	2	Devizes Town	1	(aet)
Round 1	Horsham YMCA	1	Deal Town	2	
Round 1	Ilfracombe Town	1	Plymouth Parkway	0	(aet)
Round 1	Jarrow Roofing Boldon CA	2	Crook Town	3	(aet)
Round 1	Larkhall Athletic	4	Slimbridge	0	
Round 1	Liskeard Athletic	1	Barnstaple Town	2	
Round 1	London APSA	0	Haringey & Waltham Development	3	
Round 1	Loughborough University	1	Godmanchester Rovers	2	
Round 1	Lutterworth Athletic	1	Oadby Town	2	
Round 1	Lydney Town	1	Shortwood United	2	
Round 1	Melksham Town	2	Wells City	1	(aet)
Round 1	Mildenhall Town	1	Wroxham	0	
Round 1	Molesey	3	Chichester City	4	(aet)
Round 1	Newcastle Benfield	2	Hebburn Town	1	
Round 1	Norton United	4	Heath Hayes	0	
Round 1	Old Woodstock Town	4	Abingdon Town	3	
Round 1	Oldham Boro	1	Padiham	3	
Round 1	Oxhey Jets	1	Enfield 1893	6	
Round 1	Parkgate	2	Scarborough Athletic	0	
Round 1	Peacehaven & Telscombe	3	Raynes Park Vale	1	
Round 1	Pilkington XXX	2	Boldmere St Michaels	5	
Round 1	Ramsbottom United	4	Colne	0	
Round 1	Ringmer	5	Woodstock Sports	0	
Round 1	Runcorn Linnets	2	Barnoldswick Town	3	(aet)
Round 1	Saltash United	3	Witheridge	2	
Round 1	Seaford Town	1	Tunbridge Wells	2	
Round 1	Shildon	2	West Auckland Town	3	(aet)
Round 1	Shrewton United	1	Fawley	2	
Round 1	South Park	1	Colliers Wood United	0	(aet)
Round 1	Southend Manor	2	Biggleswade United	1	
Round 1	Spalding United	2	Greenwood Meadows	1	
Round 1	Squires Gate	3	AFC Darwen	0	
Round 1	St Andrews	4	Bugbrooke St Michaels	2	(aet)
Round 1	Stafford Town	3	Atherstone Town	2	
Round 1	Stratford Town	0	Racing Club Warwick	4	
Round 1	Three Bridges	3	Beckenham Town	0	(aet)
Round 1	Tipton Town	2	Highgate United	1	(aet)
Round 1	Tividale	4	Westfields	1	
Round 1	Tring Athletic	3	Hullbridge Sports	2	
Round 1	VCD Athletic	5	Lordswood	0	
Round 1	Winslow United	2	Buckingham Town	5	
Round 1	Wisbech Town	3	Walsham Le Willows	0	(aet)
Round 1	Witney Town	2	Carterton	1	
Round 1	Woodbridge Town	1	Witham Town	1	(aet)
Replay	Consett	3	Guisborough Town	2	
Replay	Stewarts & Lloyds (2)	1	Harborough Town	0	
Replay	Witham Town	4	Woodbridge Town	1	
Round 2	Alton Town	2	Wantage Town	2	(aet)
Round 2	Ampthill Town	3	Haringey & Waltham Development	2	
Round 2	Ashington	1	Norton & Stockton Ancients	0	
Round 2	Ashville	1	Staveley MW	2	
Round 2	Barnoldswick Town	0	Spennymoor Town	5	
Round 2	Barnstaple Town	3	Downton	2	
Round 2	Bemerton Heath Harlequins	3	Saltash United	1	
Round 2	Billingham Synthonia	2	Crook Town	0	

88

Round 2	Billingham Town	2	Glossop North End	4	
Round 2	Bishop Sutton	2	Shortwood United	4	
Round 2	Bitton	3	Cullompton Rangers	2	
Round 2	Blackfield & Langley	2	VCD Athletic	3	
Round 2	Bodmin Town	1	Larkhall Athletic	1	(aet)
Round 2	Boldmere St Michaels	0	Peterborough Northern Star	2	
Round 2	Boston Town	0	Gornal Athletic	3	
Round 2	Bournemouth (Ams)	4	Torpoint Athletic	0	
Round 2	Bridlington Town	1	Gillford Park	0	
Round 2	Cadbury Heath	1	Falmouth Town	2	(aet)
Round 2	Christchurch	3	Melksham Town	1	
Round 2	Consett	4	Ramsbottom United	2	
Round 2	Deeping Rangers	5	Cogenhoe United	1	
Round 2	Diss Town	1	Buckingham Town	0	
Round 2	Dunston UTS	12	Blackwell MW	1	
Round 2	Eccleshill United	1	Armthorpe Welfare	3	
Round 2	Egham Town	0	Cowes Sports	1	
Round 2	Felixstowe & Walton United	0	Bethnal Green United	7	
Round 2	Glasshoughton Welfare	0	Runcorn Town	2	
Round 2	Godmanchester Rovers	3	Bloxwich United	2	
Round 2	Gresley	2	King's Lynn Town	0	
Round 2	Hanworth Villa	3	Deal Town	1	
Round 2	Herne Bay	3	Winchester City	1	
Round 2	Ilfracombe Town	1	Winterbourne United	0	
Round 2	Lancing	2	Guildford City (2)	1	
Round 2	Leverstock Green	0	Enfield 1893	0	(aet)
Round 2	Littlehampton Town	0	Flackwell Heath	2	
Round 2	Long Buckby	4	Dunstable Town	2	
Round 2	Long Eaton United	0	St Ives Town	3	
Round 2	Mildenhall Town	0	Sporting Bengal United	2	
Round 2	Newcastle Benfield	2	Barton Town Old Boys	1	
Round 2	Newport Pagnell Town	5	Stansted	0	
Round 2	Norton United	2	Ellesmere Rangers	1	(aet)
Round 2	Oadby Town	1	St Andrews	0	
Round 2	Old Woodstock Town	4	Witney Town	3	
Round 2	Padiham	2	Askern Villa	5	
Round 2	Pagham	2	Peacehaven & Telscombe	4	(aet)
Round 2	Parkgate	4	Bedlington Terriers	3	
Round 2	Racing Club Warwick	0	Wisbech Town	1	
Round 2	Reading Town	2	Erith Town	1	
Round 2	Ringmer	2	Binfield	2	(aet)
Round 2	Royston Town	3	Thetford Town	1	
Round 2	Rye United	1	Three Bridges	2	
Round 2	South Park	3	Fawley	0	
Round 2	Southend Manor	4	Whitton United	2	(aet)
Round 2	Spalding United	0	Tividale	3	
Round 2	Squires Gate	3	Winsford United	1	(aet)
Round 2	Stafford Town	1	Brocton	2	
Round 2	Stewarts & Lloyds (2)	0	Holbrook Sports	2	
Round 2	Tipton Town	5	Bardon Hill Sports	1	
Round 2	Tring Athletic	2	Haringey Borough	3	
Round 2	Tunbridge Wells	4	Chichester City	1	(aet)
Round 2	West Auckland Town	3	Bacup Borough	1	
Round 2	Whitley Bay	4	Tadcaster Albion	1	
Round 2	Willand Rovers	1	Highworth Town	1	(aet)
Round 2	Witham Town	3	Team Bury	1	

Replay	Binfield	0	Ringmer	0	(aet)
	Binfield won on penalties				
Replay	Enfield 1893	2	Leverstock Green	2	(aet)
	Enfield 1893 won on penalties				
Replay	Highworth Town	0	Willand Rovers	1	
Replay	Larkhall Athletic	2	Bodmin Town	1	
Replay	Wantage Town	4	Alton Town	1	
Round 3	Askern Villa	2	West Auckland Town	3	
Round 3	Bemerton Heath Harlequins	0	Shortwood United	4	
Round 3	Bethnal Green United	5	Sporting Bengal United	2	
Round 3	Billingham Synthonia	4	Consett	0	
Round 3	Binfield	3	Flackwell Heath	1	
Round 3	Bitton	3	Christchurch	0	
Round 3	Bournemouth (Ams)	2	Barnstaple Town	0	
Round 3	Dunston UTS	3	Parkgate	1	
Round 3	Glossop North End	1	Runcorn Town	2	
Round 3	Gresley	4	Gornal Athletic	2	
Round 3	Hanworth Villa	2	Herne Bay	2	(aet)
Round 3	Haringey Borough	1	Royston Town	2	
Round 3	Holbrook Sports	2	Norton United	2	(aet)
Round 3	Ilfracombe Town	1	Larkhall Athletic	1	(aet)
Round 3	Lancing	1	Ampthill Town	3	
Round 3	Larkhall Athletic	1	Ilfracombe Town	0	
Round 3	Long Buckby	1	Enfield 1893	2	
Round 3	Newcastle Benfield	3	Deeping Rangers	1	
Round 3	Newport Pagnell Town	3	Godmanchester Rovers	1	
Round 3	Oadby Town	1	Tipton Town	1	(aet)
Round 3	Old Woodstock Town	1	Wantage Town	0	
Round 3	Peacehaven & Telscombe	1	St Ives Town	2	
Round 3	Peterborough Northern Star	2	Armthorpe Welfare	0	
Round 3	Reading Town	1	Cowes Sports	0	
Round 3	South Park	2	Diss Town	1	
Round 3	Southend Manor	0	Three Bridges	0	(aet)
Round 3	Spennymoor Town	0	Ashington	2	
Round 3	Squires Gate	0	Staveley MW	4	
Round 3	Tividale	3	Brocton	3	(aet)
Round 3	VCD Athletic	3	Tunbridge Wells	3	(aet)
Round 3	Whitley Bay	5	Bridlington Town	1	
Round 3	Willand Rovers	2	Falmouth Town	1	
Round 3	Witham Town	1	Wisbech Town	2	
Replay	Brocton	1	Tividale	2	
Replay	Herne Bay	3	Hanworth Villa	1	
Replay	Norton United	2	Holbrook Sports	0	
Replay	Three Bridges	4	Southend Manor	1	
Replay	Tipton Town	1	Oadby Town	2	
Replay	Tunbridge Wells	2	VCD Athletic	0	
Round 4	Billingham Synthonia	0	Runcorn Town	0	
Round 4	Bitton	1	West Auckland Town	3	
Round 4	Bournemouth (Ams)	2	Royston Town	1	
Round 4	Gresley	1	Three Bridges	1	(aet)
Round 4	Newcastle Benfield	1	Herne Bay	2	
Round 4	Newport Pagnell Town	2	Ashington	3	
Round 4	Norton United	1	Peterborough Northern Star	2	
Round 4	Oadby Town	2	Ampthill Town	1	
Round 4	Old Woodstock Town	0	Bethnal Green United	2	
Round 4	Reading Town	2	Larkhall Athletic	3	

Round 4	Shortwood United	1	Enfield 1893	0	
Round 4	Tividale	7	Binfield	1	
Round 4	Tunbridge Wells	0	St Ives Town	1	
Round 4	Whitley Bay	5	South Park	0	
Round 4	Willand Rovers	1	Staveley MW	3	
Round 4	Wisbech Town	2	Dunston UTS	2	(aet)
Replay	Dunston UTS	3	Wisbech Town	1	
Replay	Runcorn Town	1	Billingham Synthonia	2	
Replay	Three Bridges	2	Gresley	2	(aet)
	Gresley won on penalties				
Round 5	Billingham Synthonia	0	Bournemouth (Ams)	0	(aet)
Round 5	Dunston UTS	3	Bethnal Green United	0	
Round 5	Herne Bay	1	Larkhall Athletic	0	
Round 5	Shortwood United	3	Ashington	0	
Round 5	St Ives Town	4	Gresley	0	
Round 5	Staveley MW	2	Oadby Town	0	
Round 5	Tividale	0	Peterborough Northern Star	2	(aet)
Round 5	Whitley Bay	1	West Auckland Town	2	
Replay	Bournemouth (Ams)	2	Billingham Synthonia	1	
Round 6	Bournemouth (Ams)	0	West Auckland Town	2	
Round 6	Peterborough Northern Star	3	Dunston UTS	4	(aet)
Round 6	Shortwood United	1	Herne Bay	2	
Round 6	Staveley MW	3	St Ives Town	0	
Semi-Finals					
1st leg	Dunston UTS	1	Staveley MW	0	
2nd leg	Staveley MW	2	Dunston UTS	2	
	Dunston UTS won 3-2 on aggregate				
1st leg	Herne Bay	2	West Auckland Town	2	
2nd leg	West Auckland Town	2	Herne Bay	1	
	West Auckland Town won 4-3 on aggregate				
FINAL	Dunston UTS	2	West Auckland Town	0	

Football Conference
Blue Square Premier
Fixtures
2012/2013 Season

	AFC Telford United	Alfreton Town	Barrow	Braintree Town	Cambridge United	Dartford	Ebbsfleet United	Forest Green Rovers	Gateshead	Grimsby Town	Hereford United	Hyde	Kidderminster Harriers	Lincoln City	Luton Town	Macclesfield Town	Mansfield Town	Newport County	Nuneaton Town	Southport	Stockport County	Tamworth	Woking	Wrexham
AFC Telford United	■	19/01	04/12	18/08	02/02	06/04	06/11	14/08	22/01	13/10	20/04	12/02	17/11	08/09	22/12	09/03	22/09	25/09	30/03	05/01	27/08	16/02	06/10	01/01
Alfreton Town	27/10	■	22/12	29/09	01/12	05/01	12/03	20/04	16/03	09/10	18/08	26/02	22/09	30/03	08/09	16/02	01/01	09/11	27/08	14/08	06/04	26/01	09/02	04/12
Barrow	11/08	25/08	■	20/04	29/09	13/10	23/03	17/11	26/12	04/09	07/12	01/04	01/09	10/11	02/02	29/12	06/04	15/09	16/02	09/10	22/01	02/03	12/01	26/02
Braintree Town	12/01	23/03	06/10	■	26/12	25/09	01/04	04/12	10/11	19/01	09/02	11/08	04/09	02/02	26/02	01/12	13/04	25/08	09/03	16/02	22/09	01/09	29/12	27/10
Cambridge United	15/09	12/02	13/04	01/01	■	27/08	22/01	02/03	08/12	26/01	23/02	27/10	25/09	14/08	30/03	10/11	06/10	06/04	22/12	18/08	05/01	17/11	09/03	08/09
Dartford	09/10	01/09	26/01	22/01	29/12	■	26/12	06/11	23/03	26/02	15/09	29/09	25/08	08/12	12/02	12/01	26/10	04/09	20/04	17/11	23/02	11/08	01/04	09/03
Ebbsfleet United	13/04	13/10	22/09	14/08	04/12	01/01	■	30/03	09/02	01/12	22/12	10/11	06/10	05/01	27/08	02/02	08/09	09/03	06/04	16/03	16/02	19/01	25/09	18/08
Forest Green Rovers	01/04	15/09	09/03	12/02	11/08	16/02	04/09	■	12/01	23/03	22/01	01/09	29/12	28/09	27/10	08/12	16/03	26/12	01/12	13/04	10/11	09/10	25/08	02/02
Gateshead	29/09	06/11	01/01	02/03	13/10	08/09	20/04	18/08	■	04/12	26/01	09/03	12/02	27/08	06/04	09/10	14/08	01/12	05/01	30/03	22/12	15/09	19/01	16/02
Grimsby Town	09/02	02/02	30/03	17/11	16/03	06/10	23/02	08/09	25/09	■	05/01	22/01	09/03	01/01	21/09	27/10	27/08	20/04	18/08	06/04	14/08	08/12	10/11	22/12
Hereford United	01/12	12/01	16/03	13/10	22/09	19/01	25/08	25/09	13/04	01/09	■	23/03	26/12	16/02	06/11	11/08	04/12	29/12	02/03	02/02	06/10	01/04	04/09	12/02
Hyde	08/12	25/09	14/08	06/04	19/01	16/03	26/01	05/01	06/10	06/11	08/09	■	16/02	20/04	17/08	09/02	22/12	02/03	22/09	27/08	01/01	13/10	01/12	30/03
Kidderminster Harr.	29/01	23/02	05/01	30/03	09/02	22/12	02/03	27/08	27/10	15/09	01/01	09/10	■	06/04	14/08	29/09	18/08	08/12	12/01	10/11	08/09	20/04	16/03	01/12
Lincoln City	23/03	04/09	23/02	06/11	01/04	09/02	01/09	26/01	29/12	26/12	17/11	15/09	11/08	■	06/10	25/08	26/02	12/01	25/09	09/03	27/10	13/04	04/12	19/01
Luton Town	25/08	08/12	01/12	09/10	04/09	10/11	29/12	09/02	11/08	13/04	09/03	12/01	01/04	22/01	■	01/09	23/02	16/02	13/10	29/09	26/01	23/03	26/12	15/09
Macclesfield Town	26/01	06/10	27/08	08/09	20/04	18/08	17/11	22/09	23/02	02/03	06/04	04/12	19/01	22/12	05/01	■	25/09	13/10	12/02	01/01	30/03	06/11	12/03	14/08
Mansfield Town	02/03	26/12	09/02	15/09	16/02	02/02	08/12	13/10	01/04	29/12	29/09	25/08	12/01	09/10	15/11	23/03	■	11/08	22/01	10/11	09/03	04/09	01/09	20/04
Newport County	23/02	13/04	19/01	22/12	06/11	30/03	09/10	01/01	26/02	29/09	27/08	17/11	02/02	18/08	04/12	16/03	12/02	■	14/08	22/09	08/09	09/02	27/10	05/01
Nuneaton Town	04/09	29/12	27/10	26/01	25/08	04/12	11/08	23/02	01/09	12/01	09/10	13/04	26/02	16/03	19/01	15/09	06/11	01/04	■	09/02	17/11	26/12	23/03	29/09
Southport	01/09	01/04	12/02	08/12	12/01	02/03	15/09	12/03	04/09	11/08	27/10	29/12	23/03	30/11	20/04	26/12	19/01	26/01	06/10	■	25/09	25/08	23/02	06/11
Stockport County	29/12	11/08	06/11	16/03	01/09	13/04	29/08	19/01	25/08	01/04	26/02	26/12	13/10	12/02	02/03	04/09	01/12	23/03	02/02	04/12	■	12/01	15/09	10/10
Tamworth	10/11	09/03	08/09	05/01	26/02	01/12	27/10	06/04	02/02	12/02	14/08	23/02	04/12	22/09	25/09	22/01	30/03	06/10	02/01	22/12	18/08	■	20/04	27/08
Woking	16/03	17/11	18/08	23/02	09/10	14/08	12/02	22/12	22/09	16/02	30/03	02/02	06/11	02/03	01/01	13/04	05/01	22/01	08/09	13/10	08/12	29/09	■	06/04
Wrexham	26/12	02/03	25/09	28/08	23/03	22/09	12/01	06/10	17/11	25/08	10/11	04/09	13/04	13/10	16/03	01/04	26/01	01/09	08/12	22/01	09/02	29/12	11/08	■

Please note that the above fixtures may be subject to change.

Football Conference Blue Square North Fixtures 2012/2013 Season	Altrincham	Bishop's Stortford	Boston United	Brackley Town	Bradford Park Avenue	Chester	Colwyn Bay	Corby Town	Droylsden	Gainsborough Trinity	Gloucester City	Guiseley	FC Halifax Town	Harrogate Town	Hinckley United	Histon	Oxford City	Solihull Moors	Stalybridge Celtic	Vauxhall Motors	Worcester City	Workington
Altrincham		13/04	22/12	18/08	15/09	27/08	23/02	09/02	27/04	08/12	02/02	30/10	20/10	05/01	17/11	01/09	02/03	19/01	01/01	30/03	23/03	02/10
Bishop's Stortford	29/09		27/08	30/03	20/04	13/10	06/04	01/12	23/02	17/11	23/03	05/01	18/08	22/12	16/02	01/01	30/10	04/09	02/02	08/09	19/01	09/03
Boston United	26/02	01/04		27/04	23/03	15/09	12/01	26/12	15/12	02/10	26/01	17/11	13/04	01/12	25/08	21/08	29/12	20/10	16/02	02/03	27/10	01/09
Brackley Town	15/12	25/09	09/03		12/01	08/12	26/01	01/04	01/09	20/10	29/12	06/04	27/10	09/02	21/08	02/10	26/12	16/02	17/11	23/03	20/04	15/09
Bradford Park Avenue	09/03	27/10	29/09	08/09		05/01	16/02	23/02	13/04	03/11	13/10	01/01	27/08	30/03	19/11	27/04	08/12	02/02	03/09	22/12	18/08	19/01
Chester	01/04	02/03	06/04	02/02	03/10		25/08	20/10	26/12	12/01	16/03	08/09	05/09	03/11	29/12	27/10	15/12	20/04	19/01	23/02	01/12	22/08
Colwyn Bay	16/03	09/02	08/09	29/09	30/10	30/03		02/03	19/01	13/04	27/04	04/09	22/12	08/12	13/10	17/11	23/03	18/08	27/08	01/01	05/01	02/02
Corby Town	13/10	27/02	01/01	27/08	01/09	16/02	15/09		03/10	27/04	31/10	19/01	02/02	16/03	08/12	05/01	17/11	22/12	09/03	18/08	30/03	13/04
Droylsden	03/11	08/12	18/08	05/01	02/03	01/01	27/10	06/04		09/02	29/09	09/03	16/02	04/09	26/01	20/10	20/04	08/09	30/03	27/08	22/12	23/03
Gainsborough Trinity	04/09	16/03	02/02	23/02	26/01	23/03	01/12	29/09	13/10		18/08	30/03	01/01	27/08	30/10	16/02	06/04	05/01	22/12	20/04	08/09	27/10
Gloucester City	01/12	02/10	03/11	04/09	09/02	17/11	20/10	20/04	12/02	19/01		22/12	05/01	23/02	09/03	30/03	21/08	27/08	08/09	06/04	01/01	08/12
Guiseley	26/01	15/09	09/02	02/03	26/12	13/04	29/12	15/12	21/08	25/08	01/09		03/11	18/09	27/04	08/12	12/01	16/03	02/10	27/10	20/10	01/04
FC Halifax Town	06/04	15/12	13/10	16/03	01/04	26/01	21/08	29/12	17/11	26/12	15/09	20/04		30/10	12/01	09/02	01/09	01/12	23/02	02/10	02/03	25/08
Harrogate Town	21/08	01/09	19/01	13/10	25/08	09/03	02/10	27/10	29/12	01/04	12/01	02/02	23/03		15/12	02/03	15/09	06/04	20/04	17/11	16/02	26/12
Hinckley United	20/04	20/10	30/03	22/12	06/04	09/02	29/01	23/03	16/03	02/03	27/10	01/12	08/09	18/08		27/08	02/10	01/01	05/01	19/01	03/11	23/02
Histon	29/12	26/12	20/04	19/01	01/12	26/02	09/03	03/11	02/02	15/12	25/08	18/08	29/09	08/09	01/04		23/02	30/10	06/04	13/10	04/09	12/01
Oxford City	08/09	27/04	04/09	01/01	16/03	18/08	03/11	18/09	01/12	09/03	16/02	29/09	19/01	13/04	02/02	22/12		30/03	27/10	05/01	27/08	13/10
Solihull Moors	27/10	29/12	23/02	13/04	17/11	01/09	15/12	21/08	12/01	15/09	01/04	13/10	09/03	26/01	26/12	23/03	25/08		08/12	09/02	02/10	27/04
Stalybridge Celtic	26/12	03/11	30/10	12/02	29/12	29/09	01/04	12/01	25/09	21/08	13/04	23/03	27/04	20/10	01/09	15/09	26/01	02/03		01/12	09/02	15/12
Vauxhall Motors	25/08	12/01	08/12	03/11	21/08	30/10	26/12	26/01	01/04	01/09	15/12	16/02	26/02	27/04	15/09	13/04	20/10	29/09	16/03		09/03	29/12
Worcester City	12/01	20/08	16/03	29/10	15/12	27/04	01/09	25/08	15/09	29/12	26/12	23/02	08/12	29/09	13/04	26/01	01/04	11/02	13/10	02/02		17/11
Workington	16/02	26/01	05/01	04/12	20/10	22/12	20/04	08/09	30/10	29/01	02/03	27/08	30/03	01/01	29/09	16/03	09/02	03/11	18/08	04/09	06/04	

Please note that the above fixtures may be subject to change.

Football Conference Blue Square South Fixtures 2012/2013 Season	AFC Hornchurch	Basingstoke Town	Bath City	Billericay Town	Boreham Wood	Bromley	Chelmsford City	Dorchester Town	Dover Athletic	Eastbourne Borough	Eastleigh	Farnborough	Havant & Waterlooville	Hayes & Yeading United	Maidenhead United	Salisbury City	Staines Town	Sutton United	Tonbridge Angels	Truro City	Welling United	Weston-super-Mare
AFC Hornchurch		15/12	09/03	29/12	21/08	01/04	30/10	15/09	25/08	20/10	17/11	29/09	23/03	27/04	16/02	12/01	23/02	09/02	26/01	13/04	26/12	01/09
Basingstoke Town	08/09		05/01	02/03	13/04	02/10	17/11	16/02	27/10	30/10	30/03	01/01	13/10	27/08	19/01	27/04	22/12	18/08	08/12	04/09	26/01	16/03
Bath City	27/10	23/03		01/09	29/09	15/12	16/03	29/12	15/09	01/12	13/04	03/11	25/08	13/10	21/08	01/04	02/02	27/04	16/02	23/02	12/01	26/12
Billericay Town	27/08	29/09	08/12		02/02	23/02	01/01	13/10	01/12	22/12	08/09	05/01	27/10	30/03	27/04	13/04	09/03	26/01	04/09	18/08	16/03	03/11
Boreham Wood	30/03	03/11	09/02	01/10		16/03	27/08	06/04	23/02	05/01	18/08	08/09	15/01	22/12	20/10	26/01	01/01	03/09	02/03	08/12	20/04	01/12
Bromley	04/09	09/02	08/09	17/11	16/02		22/12	02/03	27/04	30/03	05/01	08/12	29/09	13/04	30/10	27/10	18/08	01/01	27/08	09/03	13/10	26/01
Chelmsford City	19/01	20/04	06/04	26/12	29/12	25/08		15/12	01/04	03/11	13/10	01/12	12/01	02/02	23/03	01/09	27/10	23/02	09/03	29/09	20/08	15/09
Dorchester Town	16/03	01/12	27/08	26/02	09/03	20/10	08/09		03/11	18/08	04/09	22/12	26/01	05/01	13/04	09/02	30/03	08/12	27/10	04/01	29/09	27/04
Dover Athletic	22/12	06/04	02/03	30/10	17/11	19/01	04/09	20/04		27/08	08/12	18/08	09/03	08/09	29/09	20/10	05/01	30/03	01/01	02/02	09/02	04/12
Eastbourne Borough	02/02	15/09	19/02	25/08	23/03	21/08	13/04	12/01	29/12		27/10	09/03	26/12	19/01	01/09	15/12	27/04	13/10	02/10	17/11	01/04	09/02
Eastleigh	06/04	21/08	30/10	15/12	12/01	23/03	16/02	01/04	01/09	02/03		26/01	29/12	29/09	15/09	26/12	09/10	03/11	20/04	20/10	01/12	25/08
Farnborough	02/03	26/12	19/01	23/03	15/12	01/09	27/04	25/08	12/01	23/02	02/10		09/02	16/02	01/04	29/12	17/11	13/04	13/10	30/10	15/09	21/08
Havant & Waterlooville	05/01	02/02	22/12	19/01	27/04	01/12	18/08	30/10	13/04	01/01	27/08	20/10		04/09	16/03	23/02	08/12	02/03	08/09	30/03	03/11	02/10
Hayes & Yeading Utd.	01/12	29/12	26/01	21/08	25/08	03/11	20/10	23/03	15/12	20/04	23/02	27/10	01/04		26/12	15/09	02/10	09/03	07/04	09/02	01/09	12/01
Maidenhead United	02/10	23/02	30/03	09/02	26/02	20/04	05/01	17/11	26/01	08/12	09/03	04/09	06/04	01/01		01/12	27/08	22/12	18/08	08/09	27/10	13/10
Salisbury City	18/08	05/03	04/09	16/02	13/10	02/02	08/12	02/10	16/03	08/09	01/01	27/08	20/04	30/10	03/11		19/01	05/01	30/03	22/12	06/04	02/03
Staines Town	13/10	25/08	20/04	15/09	26/12	12/01	02/03	21/08	23/03	26/01	09/02	06/04	01/09	16/03	29/12	29/09		01/12	03/11	23/10	15/12	01/04
Sutton United	20/04	12/01	17/11	06/04	01/04	26/12	02/10	01/09	21/08	16/02	02/02	16/03	15/09	04/12	25/08	23/03	20/10		30/10	19/01	29/12	15/12
Tonbridge Angels	19/02	01/09	20/10	01/04	15/09	29/12	09/02	23/02	26/12	16/03	19/01	02/02	15/12	17/11	12/04	21/08	13/04	29/09		27/04	25/08	23/03
Truro City	03/11	01/04	02/10	12/01	01/09	15/09	26/01	26/12	13/10	06/04	16/03	20/04	21/08	02/03	15/12	25/08	16/02	27/10	01/12		23/03	29/12
Welling United	01/01	09/03	18/08	20/10	19/01	04/12	30/03	02/02	02/10	04/09	27/04	19/02	16/02	08/12	02/03	17/11	08/09	27/08	22/12	05/01		13/04
Weston-super-Mare	08/12	20/10	01/01	20/04	27/10	06/04	05/03	19/01	16/02	29/09	22/12	30/03	17/11	18/08	02/02	09/03	04/09	08/09	05/01	27/08	23/02	

Please note that the above fixtures may be subject to change.

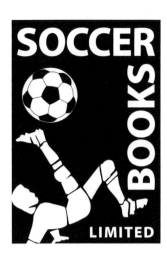

SOCCER BOOKS LIMITED

72 ST. PETERS AVENUE (Dept. SBL)
CLEETHORPES
N.E. LINCOLNSHIRE
DN35 8HU
ENGLAND

Tel. 01472 696226   Fax 01472 698546

Web site   www.soccer-books.co.uk
e-mail   info@soccer-books.co.uk

Established in 1982, Soccer Books Limited has one of the largest ranges of English-Language soccer books available. We continue to expand our stocks even further to include many more titles including German, French, Spanish and Italian-language books.

With well over 200,000 satisfied customers over the past 30 years, we supply books to virtually every country in the world but have maintained the friendliness and accessibility associated with a small family-run business. The range of titles we sell includes:

YEARBOOKS – All major yearbooks including many editions of the Sky Sports Football Yearbook (previously Rothmans), Supporters' Guides, Playfair Annuals, South and North & Central American Yearbooks, Non-League Club Directories, Almanack of World Football.

CLUB HISTORIES – Complete Statistical Records, Official Histories, Definitive Histories plus many more including photographic books.

WORLD FOOTBALL – World Cup books, European Championships History, Statistical histories for the World Cup, European Championships, South American and European Club Cup competitions and foreign-language Season Preview Magazines for dozens of countries.

BIOGRAPHIES & WHO'S WHOS – of Managers and Players plus Who's Whos etc.

ENCYCLOPEDIAS & GENERAL TITLES – Books on Stadia, Hooligan and Sociological studies, Histories and hundreds of others, including the weird and wonderful!

DVDs – Season reviews for British clubs, histories, European Cup competition finals, World Cup matches and series reviews, player profiles and a selection of almost 60 F.A. Cup Finals with many more titles becoming available all the time.

For a current printed listing of a selection of our titles, please contact us using the information at the top of this page.

Alternatively our web site offers a secure ordering system for credit and debit card holders and Paypal users and lists our full range of around 2,000 new books and over 400 DVDs.

Supporters' Guides Series

This top-selling series has been published since 1982 and the new 2013 editions contain the 2011/2012 Season's results and tables, Directions, Photographs, Telephone numbers, Parking information, Admission details, Disabled information and much more.

THE SUPPORTERS' GUIDE TO PREMIER & FOOTBALL LEAGUE CLUBS 2013

This 29th edition covers all 92 Premiership and Football League clubs. *Price £7.99*

NON-LEAGUE SUPPORTERS' GUIDE AND YEARBOOK 2013

This 21st edition covers all 68 clubs in Step 1 & Step 2 of Non-League football – the Football Conference National, Conference North and Conference South. *Price £7.99*

SCOTTISH FOOTBALL SUPPORTERS' GUIDE AND YEARBOOK 2013

The 20th edition featuring all Scottish Premier League, Scottish League and Highland League clubs. *Price £7.99*

RYMAN FOOTBALL LEAGUE SUPPORTERS' GUIDE AND YEARBOOK 2012

The 2nd edition features the 66 clubs which make up the 3 divisions of the Isthmian League, sponsored by Ryman. *Price £6.99*

EVO-STIK SOUTHERN FOOTBALL LEAGUE SUPPORTERS' GUIDE AND YEARBOOK 2012

This 2nd edition features the 66 clubs which make up the 3 divisions of the Southern League, sponsored by Evo-Stik. *Price £6.99*

EVO-STIK NORTHERN PREMIER LEAGUE SUPPORTERS' GUIDE AND YEARBOOK 2012

The 2nd edition features the 67 clubs which make up the 3 divisions of the Northern Premier League, sponsored by Evo-Stik. *Price £6.99*

THE SUPPORTERS' GUIDE TO WELSH FOOTBALL 2011

The enlarged 12th edition covers the 112+ clubs which make up the top 3 tiers of Welsh Football. *Price £8.99*

These books are available UK & Surface post free from –

Soccer Books Limited (Dept. SBL)
72 St. Peter's Avenue
Cleethorpes, DN35 8HU
United Kingdom